TAKEN

Dedicated to my own special "angel," my mother-in-law Millie Turner.

Also by Karla Turner

INTO THE FRINGE

Cover Art: *Triality* by Casey Turner © 1994

TAKEN

INSIDE
THE ALIEN-HUMAN
ABDUCTION AGENDA

KARLA TURNER, Ph.D.

First published 1994
© Karla Turner 1994

First Edition, First Printing, April 1994

Printed in the United States of America at
Rose Printing Company, Inc., Tallahassee, Florida

Library of Congress Catalog Card Number: 94-75771

ISBN 0-9640899-0-4

KELT WORKS
Post Office Box 32, Roland, Arkansas 72135

CONTENTS

iii

FOREWORD

When Karla Turner asked me to write a foreword for her new book, TAKEN, she knew that in my own work as a documentary filmmaker, television producer and author I have been struggling to see a bigger picture behind many anomalous phenomena that affect our planet. My own investigations have included mysterious worldwide crop formations, animal mutilations, and the human abduction syndrome. I am convinced that humanity is moving from the paradigm that we are alone in the universe to a new one in which we are not alone and something out there is interacting with us, our animals, and our plant life, forcing glimpses of other realities upon us.

The true nature and purpose of the intelligence, or intelligences, remains an enigma. The eight women in this book report communications ranging from telepathic thoughts to virtual reality dreams, but there is no coherent single truth that emerges from their experiences, nor from the hundreds of others in the abduction syndrome since the 1960s. The sheer number of different messages, often contradictory, produces confusion, mistrust and a sense of manipulation, even if that manipulation inspires positively or disturbs negatively.

"Perfectly real aliens exist out there," says one of the women in TAKEN, "and it seems one kind wants to help us and another kind wants to deceive us."

As each voice is offered for public consideration, there are themes that repeat. One of the most prominent is genetic harvesting from earth life to create a hybrid species. TAKEN suggests the possibility that an alien intelligence has been using genetic manipulation to create evolving species on our planet over eons and that *Homo sapiens sapiens* might be one such genetically engineered species. If so, we on the Petri dish might paradoxically be trying to study whatever watches and studies us. Consciousness of this Other without running from it or getting down on our knees to it could be a significant, perhaps unexpected, step in human evolution and survival.

Linda Moulton Howe,
Creator and Supervising TV Producer,
UFO Report: Sightings and author of
An Alien Harvest and *Glimpses of
Other Realities*

pROLOGUE

Indiana, 1954...

"They came in our house and set up equipment in the living room," Pat said. "The Army men wanted to talk to me the most. Me, an eleven-year-old girl with secrets in my head. But the aliens told me I couldn't tell because 'there will be those who will tamper with your mind.' And here they were, the tamperers, the Army men."

Two female doctors set up their gear in the bedroom, where Pat was given an injection. "It made me sleepy," she said, "and I lay on my mom's bed on some towels and told them my story. I even told them, 'You're in my mom's room where the White, glowing ones were. You don't belong here, but they do'."

Puerto Rico, 1978...

Two aliens took Beth down a curved hall and through a door, into a different area. It looked like "a surgery room," and she became afraid they were going to kill her there. A third entity, holding a black box, moved to a position behind Beth. She could not see what he did, but she felt as if her head was being opened and her brain removed, all without any sensation of pain. After she was "all put back together again," a cold liquid was poured over her head.

When this procedure was finished, the aliens stood in front of her, and Beth realized that mentally she was different. Her thoughts about everything were changed, and she was filled with new ideas about God and the unity of all life within that supreme source.

This very spiritual moment was followed by a quite physical exam, as the aliens took samples from her skin and hair. A human-looking man with a widow's-peak hairline entered and made a full examination of her body, including a gynecological procedure. Then he explained many things, telling her that she and other humans had been "chosen" to carry out certain "jobs" in the future.

Texas, 1992...
"The masked alien explained that her race had been doing things to humans that they should not be doing," Amy said. "She and several groups of her race, and others, wanted to stop the 'abuse' of the humans by her race. They were working with certain people on Earth to stop the process. The other humans in the room were ex-pilots, military officials, and other professionals. They were all working together to stop the alien intrusions.

"She showed me the thing she had pulled out of my neck and said, 'This is embedded deep in the spinal cord.' The thing controlled the muscles of the body when activated. It blocked the brain and became the 'central command' of the body. I don't want to remember how or why this thing functioned."

1

REDEFINITION

Like Pat, Beth, and Amy, I am an abductee. I have been forcibly taken and controlled by non-human entities. When I told my story of alien encounters in INTO THE FRINGE, I was contacted by these women and many other people with similar experiences, in need of support and assistance.

I am also a researcher of abduction reports, and from these contacts emerged a number of accounts that shed important light on the alien agenda of human interaction. This book is the result of lengthy investigations into the abduction experiences of eight women from various parts of the country. The correlation of evidence from their accounts greatly widens the parameters of the abduction scenario and points to certain aspects, previously disregarded or avoided, in need of serious exploration.

This is also a personal book, a collation of unique, intimate accounts of alien-human interactions. The people who share their experiences here are courageous representatives of the many others in this country and elsewhere whose lives partake of parallel realities. They function successfully in a world shared by everyone else, as housewives, mothers, grandmothers, artists, nurses, counselors, teachers, computer engineers, and blue-collar workers.

But in the blink of an eye—or the flash of

multicolored lights strobing in the hall late at night–
their normal lives can disappear, and they find
themselves taken into the time and space of an alien
world.

It is difficult for most abduction memories to be
investigated in a purely scientific manner, especially
since they are often suppressed, surfacing only as
vague flashbacks and dreamlike episodes. In this field
there has been strong objection to anecdotal
information. But the scientific approach to the study
of the UFO phenomenon as a whole has proven less
than successful. In spite of half a century of many
intelligent people researching the UFO and alien
presence with scientific methods, reliable answers to
the primary questions have not been found.
Investigations of sightings reports, landing traces,
photos and video tapes, alleged implants, and related
government documents have amassed a mountain of
data and a number of theories–but nothing
indisputably true about the nature of UFOs and their
non-human occupants, their origin, or the reason for
their presence here among us now.

Great gains have been made in the area of
abduction therapy, providing help and support for
those who are living with the phenomenon and
working to resolve their emotional trauma, to keep
the disruption of their everyday lives to a minimum,
and to transform or assimilate these experiences in a
positive way. And while is this laudable, it is not
necessarily research. Therapy's goal is one of personal
balance, but the goal of research is a larger, clearer
understanding of the phenomenon. The point is not
so much learning to live with abductions as it is
finding out why they happen, what they mean, and

whether and how the situation can be altered.

The need for reliable answers is nowhere greater than in the abduction phenomenon. It intimately affects people of all ages and backgrounds, irrevocably altering their personal lives and their perceptions of reality, and it raises immense questions about our past, present, and future as a species. But in spite of the best scientific approaches to the question, all that ufological research has brought to most people is a realization that UFOs exist–and perhaps a few cute, harmless aliens–but no confrontation with what this means.

Science has been trying to measure a dream, it seems, using traditional ideas and practices, and it has proved elusive. The UFO phenomenon is not confined to our current scientific understanding of perceived reality. We do not yet have the technology or natural perceptive abilities to capture and assess it. That is why the scientific approach to photographic evidence, landing traces, implants, and document analyses has so little in the way of hard evidence to show for its work. Instead, its best results offer only circumstantial data, carrying very little more weight than the anecdotal data of abduction research in the scales of traditional science.

It is in the abduction phenomenon that we come most urgently face to face with the alien presence and thus have our best opportunity to observe the activity and assess its purpose or agenda. All of the UFO photos in the world tell us nothing compared to the words of those who have encountered the alien force in their lives and those of their families.

And there are many, like Pat and Amy and the others presented here. From the response to INTO

THE FRINGE, it sometimes seemed that abduction experiences were becoming virtually epidemic. Yet studies by mental health professionals show that the people who make these reports are eminently sane, that the aftermath of these events is real, and that they do not spring from any mass psychosis but from *experienced* anomalous trauma.

I also found that many of the reports contained details very similar to certain things my family and I had experienced. Still, in every case there was always present the "unique factor" within the situations, providing highly individualized episodes for each abductee. I often wondered if these unique events, these "one-time shots," might not prove to have some unperceived correlations, to form a pattern as yet out of focus, and give us more information than the now-recognized patterns of certain exams, baby presentations, and the like. Far from being a neat, limited phenomenon, alien interaction with humans is still very much a riddle, mystery, enigma, and more.

Abduction research has not yet produced answers, but there are certainly different theories to be had–an embarrassment of riches, really. Unfortunately, these theories rest on a very partial, highly selective use of the data, rather than dealing with the complexities of the entire, life-long and minute-by-minute, reality of the abduction scenario.

It is more than the sum of its parts. The intermittent UFO sightings, missing-time episodes, conscious encounters, and virtual-reality scenarios are like blank milestones on a journey which, for the abductee, is continuous and headed in an unknown direction. More accurately, they are like lights that suddenly appear in the dark, which we hope will shed illumination and lead to understanding. Instead, however, these startling lights either blind us with their intensity, so that we cannot see their source, or they cast strange shadows, whose false appearances and misleading movements can easily confuse and disorient us.

No one knows this better than an abductee. Investigators who have not had personal experiences with the phenomenon can listen to abduction accounts and then ponder the possibilities. Was the person lying? Was it a real event, or did it occur on a mental level? What parts of the recollection are real, and which are illusionary? But the abductee understands that it may very well be both possibilities at once, both real and mental, real and illusionary. The aliens, whether by intellectual, psychic, or technological means, are able to create any perception, and therefore any illusion, for the person in their hands.

The implications are explosive. Perhaps that is why the logical conclusions of these implications are so rarely taken into account. If we credit the idea of illusionary mastery with serious validity, then we must either come up with a reliable acid test to discern illusion and actuality in abduction events, or we may have to admit that the truth behind these events is unknowable in current scientific terms. Dealing with the aliens' deceptive abilities may be the most crucial problem facing abduction research today.

Once the illusionary capability has been demonstrated and experienced, new perceptions and insights often emerge. The witness usually has no trouble recognizing the non-human nature of the force behind the events. The manipulation of time and space by these beings, the way they play with our psychology and our perceptions, all bespeak a technology far beyond the human. Or certainly, if any human agency did have this sort of capability, it would have plenty of applications far better than pulling hundreds of 3 a.m. raids on bedrooms around the globe every night, decade after decade, in which thousands of humans pretend to be aliens.

The abductee also learns from experience that the aliens induce an altered perceptive state in humans during every encounter. Employed for control, it can be used to prevent any undesired responses from the abductee. And the altered state prevents any objective assessment of the situation by the witness. This means that the witness can only report what was seen, felt, and heard–which is not necessarily a reflection of what actually occurred. By inducing and manipulating altered consciousness in the abductee, the aliens assume full control of the situation and thus exert great control over the data reported by the witness.

Abductees report alien-controlled information.

This is a fact abduction researchers must face. Then, perhaps, work can begin on solving this problem, on finding ways around the memory blocks and screen illusions, in order to discover the real events and the agenda behind them. Until the day we can unmask the alien illusions, however, we can at least study the entire body of reported data, controlled though it may be, trying to learn more about why certain images and events are employed and what they can tell us about the covert directors of these scenarios.

Many of the people who contacted me after reading INTO THE FRINGE are looking for answers, just as I am compelled to do. This present work is an attempt to aid in the search, making a number of representative cases available for public scrutiny and assessment. Too often, reports on abduction activity are presented entirely in second-hand form by investigators, and too often these reports are incomplete, focusing only on some parts of an event and discarding or ignoring others.

Such omissions are clearly a hindrance to research, for the censored reports cannot present a total picture of the abduction phenomenon. It must include a real feeling for what it is like to live with such events. Abductees operate in parallel realities, searching for the strength to cope with the real and the unreal at the same time because, as they have learned, one can never be sure which is which in this phenomenon.

The number of abduction reports around the country shows just how widespread the phenomenon may be, and the numbers continue to increase. Eight different abductees, all women, from various parts of the country have volunteered to share their experiences here. Born between 1943 and 1966, they live in five different states and Puerto Rico. They were unacquainted with one another at the time of their contacts with me. Their backgrounds are as varied as their occupations, and so are their ideas about the abduction phenomenon.

Like most of us who've had alien encounters, these women are uncertain about the nature of the events they've reported. They have many questions and very few answers. Four of the women have never undergone regressive hypnosis and thus are only reporting events they consciously recalled. The other four women have used hypnosis, although very minimally as will be noted in their accounts, and almost everything in their reports also comes from conscious, pre-hypnosis, recollections.

I point this out because there are some who have raised doubts and questions about the use of regressive hypnosis in abduction research. Some feel that hypnotically retrieved information is no more reliable than conscious recollections; some believe that the use of hypnosis can contaminate and damage an investigation; and some have said they believe hypnotically retrieved information is far more reliable in abduction situations than the witness's conscious memories. The presentation here provides access to both types of data, but the majority comes from conscious recollections.

Although I believe it is extremely useful to employ regressive hypnosis in the retrieval of this information, I also think it is important to present accounts from women whose knowledge and understanding of their situations is gleaned only from the incomplete, ambiguous memories of events they have consciously retained. Their stories and their lives are much more representative of a "typical" abductee's situation than are the accounts of those who have benefited from hypnosis, simply because most abductees have no access to this tool.

The women are not seeking notoriety, and in order to protect them from public harassment, pseudonyms have been used. But all of the details are accurate, and as bizarre as they may seem, it is important to remember that they are very real to the people involved, that in many instances there have been more than one witness to the events, as well as other corroborative evidence, and that they are highly consistent with numerous abduction reports.

These women have shared their stories because they understand the gravity of the phenomenon and hope to contribute their information to its research. They also understand the need for support which many silent abductees are experiencing. The self-doubt, isolation, even fear that result from living with alien encounters can sometimes be severe, and the need to forge bonds of mutual understanding and support is vital. These, then, are the motivations of the eight women. My own purpose is similar, which is why an update of the experiences my husband and I have witnessed is also included.

An overview of all our experiences, as well as reports of other abductees, shows a much more complex program of activity in the phenomenon than is usually acknowledged. To begin with, the abduction scenario comprises a number of different types of events. On the most immediate level are the physical abductions, in which a person is forcibly removed from the normal environment by 'alien' (in the most generic sense) entities, the person's awareness is altered, and some interaction occurs. Subsequent conscious memories of the event are usually quite incomplete. Only when the event is witnessed by more than one person, or when there are physical marks on the abductee's body–punctures, scoops, patterns of bruises, artificial designs–does the witness usually feel safe in asserting the 'reality' of the encounter.

To complicate matters, many reports show that

some interactions occur on a mental rather than a physical level. One type is an artificially induced virtual-reality scenario (VRS), an externally introduced event, that to the witness is practically indistinguishable from objective reality. The person may experience a situation with full sensory input and react with genuine physical and emotional responses, although in 'reality' the person may be lying immobile on an exam table, or sitting attached to some alien apparatus, or even asleep in bed with no outward sign of disturbance.

While the VRS may have been a matter of theory in the past, a possible explanation for some of the more "unacceptable" abduction accounts, it has now been confirmed in a three-witness, conscious event. It came to light when I was investigating the abduction experiences of Ted Rice, a psychic of excellent reputation throughout the southern states.

Ted witnessed a virtual-reality scenario when he was in Florida visiting a friend, Marie, along with another house guest, Amelia. The two women occupied twin beds in one room, and Ted slept down the hall in another. Not long after going to bed one night during his visit, he was awakened by Marie shouting for him to "come quickly!"

Heading down the hall, Ted saw a pervasive blue glow emanating from the other bedroom doorway. Entering, he found Marie pressed against the far wall, staring at the twin beds in shock.

And he saw where the blue light was coming from. Amelia lay immobile in one bed, surrounded by a huge, blue, glowing, "electrical" sphere of light. Her eyes were open, and she didn't seem to be in any distress as she carried on a conversation with someone Ted and Marie couldn't see. Terrified, they tried to talk to her, but they could hardly hear one another even when shouting. Amelia continued to speak within the sphere for several minutes, until the blue light suddenly disappeared, at which point she was finally free of the paralysis that had kept her in the bed.

Amelia told Ted and Marie that the experience started with the loud sound of a helicopter low over the house. When she opened her eyes she could see through the ceiling and roof, as if they'd disappeared, to where the helicopter was hovering just above the house. She described two entities in the craft, whom she said also appeared at the foot of the bed before the blue light vanished. One being was tall, with greenish skin, an egg-shaped head, and slanted eyes as the only visible facial features. The other, shorter, entity, Amelia said, was blue-black in color.

Ted and Marie had seen absolutely nothing of these creatures, nor had they heard a helicopter at any time. But they had seen the sphere of light, with brighter, darting lights shooting through it, and Amelia frozen in a slightly raised position inside it, for she had been starting to sit up when the light coalesced and paralyzed her.

Amelia's perception of the experience was completely "real" for her. She was conscious when it began and throughout the entire event, as Ted and Marie attested. From everything her sensory input told her, Amelia had experienced an actual event with the craft and entities. Virtual reality. And the conscious and unaffected witnesses, Ted and Marie, observed objectively real effects of the mechanism which manipulated the event, verifying its external origin.

VRS technology exists and is in use, this much is clear. And unless there are outside witnesses, such as in this rare instance, the experiencer cannot personally discern between a VRS and an actual event. The virtual-reality scenario may occur while the person is conscious, as in Amelia's case, or it may be introduced into the person's dream state. According to those who've experienced the VRS dream—and I am one of those, as will be discussed later—it is an intrusive event that suddenly interrupts a normal dream. The experiencer is aware of a total, abrupt change in consciousness and finds himself in an event altogether different from his dream.

What follows may be a perceived event, with action, location, and personnel, or it may be a communication or even a vision. At its conclusion, the experiencer normally awakens, and, finding himself in his own bed, he rationalizes the whole thing as an extraordinary dream, in spite of the event's decidedly non-dreamlike qualities. Without physical proof of the event's reality, or even a name for this altered perceptive experiential event, he is left to call it a dream.

In addition to the abductions and virtual-reality scenarios, abductees also report telepathic contacts from entities who are not physically or perceivably present. These contacts include messages about spiritual matters, warnings of future disasters, "teaching" sessions, displays of symbols, and information on mathematics, physics, religion, politics, and the nature of the human species.

On a secondary level, there are events that occur, not during encounters, but subsequent to them, affecting things in the abductee's normal environment. Lights and electronic equipment malfunction; voices and unexplained sounds are heard; animals are physiologically affected; lights appear both inside and outside the house; there are odd and disturbing phone calls; and sometimes traces of a UFO's presence or landing on the property.

And finally there are the internal changes that take place with most abductees, reshaping their attitudes, belief structures, and perceptions of reality. Thus, the externally induced, temporary, altered awareness which occurs during abductions is paralleled by a permanent, internal alteration, and the abductee's life is forever changed.

There is much more to the abduction phenomenon than the public has been told, and this book is in part an attempt to correct that situation and expand our definition of the abduction scenario. Its primary purpose is not to offer scientific data or to convince a disbelieving audience that UFOs and aliens exist. People are coming to this awareness on their own, one by one, as the phenomenon intrudes into their lives and shatters their old reality in a way that cannot be imagined until it is experienced.

The following accounts from Pat, Polly, Lisa, Anita, Beth, Jane, Angie, and Amy show what it is like to live with this awareness far more thoroughly than any scientific analysis can hope to do. By allowing entrance into their lives, they permit others to witness the events from the inside rather than from a distance. Their experiences, while individually unique, taken together make a choir of voices expressing the range and intensity of life in the altered world of the alien abduction agenda.

13

11

pɅʈ

My investigation with Pat began when a mutual acquaintance heard her story of an unusual UFO event and suggested she contact me. A fifty-year-old divorced mother of grown children, Pat lives in Florida, but the story she related concerned an event that occurred in 1954 when she lived in Floyd's Knob, Indiana.

Pat's memory of this event, as in the case of so many people who have had UFO experiences, was totally suppressed after the occurrence. It all came flooding back into her consciousness in 1986–scenes of a brilliant orange ball of light, little gray entities both inside and outside the farmhouse, and, most disturbing of all, military personnel on the property.

"I thought I must be crazy when these memories came back, " Pat said. "But they were so strong and real, I finally got in touch with my brother and sister and asked if they recalled anything similar. My sister Rose said she recalled the aliens and the military people, too. But although my brother didn't remember the orange ball of light, he clearly remembered the military personnel and some of his interactions with them."

Through extensive conversations, letters, and drawings from Pat and her siblings, the following extraordinary scenario emerged, raising serious questions not only about the nature of the alien abduction agenda but also about the involvement of our military with citizens who have been the target of such interactions.

The setting was a sixteen-acre farm near Floyd's Knob, Indiana, in the summer of 1954. Eleven-year-old Pat lived there with her mother, step-father, grandmother, a nine-year-old brother and six-year-old sister. One night several family members saw a large orange ball of light appear outside the farmhouse. Pat had already gone to bed but was awakened by either her grandmother or her sister to look out the window. In the sky she saw the orange light sitting motionless at first, then moving rapidly out of sight around the back of the house.

"I remember vaguely thinking, *I will go back to bed to wait*. It seems to me that I knew 'they' were coming," Pat said. "I saw my mother running to the kitchen door to make sure it was locked and to see the ball come over the yard. I remember thinking, *It won't do any good to lock the door, they can come in anyway*. It was as if I 'knew' what to expect." Pat suddenly felt sleepy but didn't remember going back to bed. Her next memory was of a multicolored light slowly spinning around the room in total silence, emitting blue, purple, and violet hues. She got out of bed and went to the window where she saw a Gray floating just outside.

Look at those eyes! she thought. *They can film us!* The gaze of the Gray seemed to penetrate her entire being, and she sensed a familiarity with him.

Do not be afraid, it communicated to Pat. *You are the chosen child. We will not harm you.*

Pat turned around and saw several taller white entities coming into the bedroom. As they began to float her grandmother out of the door, Pat sensed the older woman's terror, and she, too, was feeling fearful. When the room was filled with the strange beings, a sparkling shaft of light came down through the ceiling. As it coalesced, Pat saw in the midst of the light a figure which she perceived as a blond-haired, blue-eyed Jesus, in a resplendent robe. He took Pat's right hand and said, *Do not be afraid, my child. These are mine*, gesturing to the beings who were standing all around the room.

The Jesus figure looked at Pat and said, *I am the light of the world*. Then he was again surrounded by the sparkling shaft of light, which ascended back into the ceiling and took him with it.

She and her grandmother were floated out of the room by the entities. Passing by her mother's bedroom, Pat saw a brilliant white light coming out of the room. Five of the taller Whites were around her step-father's bed, and they seemed to be examining one of his atrophied legs, the result of polio. A glowing green bar of light, about five inches long, floated over him. Continuing on through the house and out into the yard, Pat saw a bright crystalline flying craft hovering low to the ground. A beam of light came out of the bottom of the craft and engulfed her.

"I remember my sister's blonde curly head next to mine as we went up inside the craft," Pat said. "We were looking down at the ground and saw my mom and grandmother there looking up, like zombies." She could also see that the entire yard was swarming with Grays hurrying about the area. Although neither she nor Rose is certain of the exact sequence of events, they recalled a group of the smaller gray beings near

16

a ditch beside the cellar door. Rose saw the beings in a line, walking across a board spanning the ditch. But Pat's memory included a line or wall of fire in the ditch and a row of "small, gray, skinny" aliens wearing "Chinese rice-paddy hats with big brims."

"I was on one side of the long ditch, and they were on the other. They were mentally telling me *Pass through the light, it will not burn you*–which I was thinking at that time, that I would get burned. The fire was not hot, and it was supposed to cleanse me. I did go through it to the other side, but I do not remember doing it or what happened after that."

After the light transported her and Rose up into the craft, Pat recalled sitting on a table in a room with Grays present. A taller White came over with a file-type instrument and scraped skin from her inner forearm and the bottoms of her feet, clipped some of her hair, and then peeled away samples of her fingernails.

"What do you need all those pieces of me for?" she asked.

We are making a new you, the entity replied.

"Are you an angel?" Pat inquired.

Yes, the entity told her, *but not like you have been taught*.

Pat was taken into another room where she lay on a table, above which was a dark instrument. One of the Grays came in and pulled down a tube from this device which had a thin needle on the end. Pat became afraid, but the Gray told her, *This is the part you don't have to remember*. Pat knew that the needle was about to be inserted up into her right nostril, but before it happened she passed out.

Pat recalled another event during the physical

exam, being "fused" with a silver light. "It was done from something over my body," she said, "up high in the room. He [alien] 'fused me' into my head with the silver light; it will keep me from violent harm; it let me be perfect in human form for a few seconds; it was a protective light. I get the idea that when this silver light goes into my 'other body' I will be made into the 'new me.' In other words, the 'new me' will come to life with my soul in it."

Pat came back to consciousness after the episode with the needle and found herself back in the first room on the table. She was crying because she couldn't stay with the Grays. When they told her, *It isn't time yet*, she asked for a souvenir as proof that the experience had really occurred: the green "healer" rock she'd seen above her step-father's body. Although the aliens apparently gave her this device, they told her that it would not "work" properly for her, only for them. She was also told, *You are going to have to forget this.*

"Why?" Pat asked.

Because there are those who will tamper with your mind, the Gray replied.

Pat was returned to the house, where she saw all of her family sitting in the living room in a daze. "They looked like zombies," Pat said. Even her step-father was propped up on the floor leaning against a sofa. She was placed in her bed and saw one of the Grays outside her window gesturing a farewell. She responded with a wave and was immediately asleep again.

The next day, there doesn't seem to have been any discussion about the previous night's extraordinary events. But Pat's brother recalls that it was that day when the military personnel arrived. A white staff car, a green car, a jeep, and several white vans came onto the property carrying instruments and equipment. There was also a troop carrier with soldiers who proceeded to comb over the entire sixteen acres of the farm. The large truck was hidden in the barn, and Pat's brother said that he had to move the animal feed to the smokehouse because the soldiers wouldn't let him into the barn once their equipment was stored there.

"They came in our house and set up equipment in the living room," Pat recalled. "The army men wanted to talk to me the most, me, an eleven-year-old girl with secrets in my head. But the beings told me I couldn't tell because 'there will be those who will tamper with your mind.' And here they were, the tamperers, the army men."

Everyone except her brother–who was allowed to go out in order to take care of the farm animals–was kept inside the house for the four days in which the military personnel were present. Only her brother saw what was going on outside the house. He remembers more than twenty soldiers brought in the big truck and told to man their stations on the farm. Two of the men stayed at the end of the driveway, and the others performed various duties on the grounds.

When he was allowed outside to take care of the chores, Pat's brother remembers being questioned by a man dressed in a white lab coat, who asked about the chickens and pigs.

"Are your pigs out there?" the man asked, gesturing, and the boy nodded affirmatively.

"Have the pigs been acting funny?"

"No," the boy said, "why?"

The man said something about the minerals in the soil making the animals act strangely. Pat's brother said he felt comfortable with this man and wasn't afraid to answer his questions or to ask some of his own. He even asked if the man wanted some fresh mint, a favorite treat, from a patch near the cellar.

But the man refused. "They're taking samples there and we'll be in the way," he explained. "When they're done, we'll go get some."

Pat said she was "mad" about being restricted. "I felt scared like they would take away my family and put me somewhere like in a jail or something. But I also felt protected by the being who was my friend. I was calling him a little boy then, but I knew the being wasn't a real little boy."

Two female doctors set up their gear in the parents' bedroom, where Pat was given an injection. "It made me sleepy," she said, "and I lay on my mom's bed on some towels and told them my story. I even told them, 'You're in my mom's room where the white glowing ones were. You don't belong here, but they do'."

I asked Pat to start back at the beginning and tell me everything she could remember about this event. She put herself back into an eleven-year-old frame of mind and began to relive the situation.

"I see this man dressed up in a uniform of some kind, a full-dress uniform, but it is brown," she said. "He has on a coat jacket and pants that match and what I call a captain's hat. He is talking to my mother and grandmother, holding a file envelope in his hands. He has thick silver-gray hair. There is another man in a dress uniform, and he took off his coat and rolled up his sleeves. His name is Mr. Donaldson. He's an army man, too," she explained, "but the other people are setting up a 'three-TV-screen' thing in our living room. It's a little taller than I was."

Mr. Donaldson then opened out "arms" on the machine and told Pat that the device looked like a robot. "See, Pat," he said, "if we open the panels out, they look like arms, so maybe you saw a robot like this?"

"No," Pat told him adamantly, "I didn't see a robot. I saw a real little boy."

She recalled the "lady doctors" clearly. "One lady had on a white coat," she described. "One was named Dr. Susan, and she had on a light orange coat. Dr. Susan seemed to have brown-blonde hair with bangs over her forehead, and the rest of her hair was pulled back away from her face. She had what looked like stuff from a dentist's office set up in my mom's room. It had instruments of some kind on it, but it is not clear what they were. The really clear picture is of the shot thing. It was wrapped in cellophane or plastic, and there was this little hose that went with it. Both the shot thing and the hose were in the same clear plastic bag. Dr. Susan began to open the shot bag, and I got scared and asked her if I had to get a shot with that thing."

Dr. Susan then directed Pat to Mr. Donaldson, who was in the living room, speaking angrily to some men dressed in what she described as "white moon suits" holding "white metal boxes without handles." He was saying, "I told you to use the ones with the handles."

Pat said the shot made her feel "dreamy" and willing to talk about her "secret" memories." She was

21

upset that Mr. Donaldson didn't believe her. "I always told the truth," Pat said, "because my mom hated a liar, so in my wide-eyed innocence I told the army men about my visit with the beings. And I cried when they told me I didn't see what I thought I saw. They treated me like I was lying about it. After I cried, I guess Mr. Donaldson felt sorry for me because everyone started being 'sugar' nice. But I didn't like that at all because I knew it was fake. Why did they say I didn't see the little boy? Why did such a wonderful thing as this visit get everyone so upset and mad? And why did I have to get a shot?"

Someone asked about the glowing white beings and Pat said they were angels.

"How do you know they are angels?" her interrogator asked.

"Because they told me so," Pat replied.

"And what else did they tell you, Pat? Did they tell you anything else?"

"Yes," Pat answered, "they told me a lot of things, but I can't remember now. Someday I will remember, but not now."

"Why can't you remember now?" she was asked.

"Because ," Pat replied, "they said it's not time to remember, and besides, you were coming here, and I can't tell you because it's a special thing. When I'm a lot older I'll remember what they said and what's going to happen."

"Did they tell you what's going to happen?"

"Yes, they did, they told me about the 'bad time on earth.' I'm not supposed to tell about that. I can't remember now. Well," she admitted, "some of it I remember, like the crystalline ship they were in. It was full of lights, and I called it the crystalline ship because it wasn't metal like a plane. The lights made everything work by itself, and they move things without touching them, and even me, they moved me without touching me. They moved me up and down, and they are full of love, and they protected me with a silver light in me, and I love them."

One of the army men then asked her to describe the little boy's hair and clothes. Pat said she felt as if the army man was dumb, asking such a question. "Don't you know," she told him, "that the beings don't have hair and they don't wear clothes? The little boy has real big, slanty eyes that can film everything inside me, in my head and my soul. He talks to me in my head and doesn't use his mouth because he only has a line there. He's really skinny, but he doesn't have to eat because he's an angel.

"I thought angels had wings, and I laughed because he laughed with his eyes because he knew what I was thinking about the wings. I got kind of scared because I knew he was really an angel then. He knew what I thought, and only angels can tell what you think all the time, except so can Jesus. So I thought in my head, *Do you know Jesus?* and the beings and I filled up with a 'love' feeling that kind of made me cry and 'know' something special. And the being said, *Yes* in my head. I said, *Are you like the angels?* And the being said, *Yes, but not as you have been taught.* I wanted to stay with them and go back with them."

"Pat, stop for a minute," the interrogator interrupted, "and let us ask you a question. You said you wanted to go back with them? Where did you want to go back to?"

"I can't tell you that," Pat replied, "I'm not

23

supposed to tell that part. But the angel said when it was time to go they would come back, they promised me. I made them promise me. I made them promise not to forget me and I begged them to take me, but he said it wasn't time yet. I begged and cried and felt real sad. Mr. Donaldson asked me why I was crying, and I told him, 'Because you're making me cry and you're making me tell, and I'm not supposed to tell, and you think I'm lying, but I'm not."

"Okay, stop crying, Pat," Mr. Donaldson told her. "Calm down and listen to my voice. I don't think you're lying, and we won't ask you any more questions if you tell us about your souvenirs. Where are they, Pat? Do you have souvenirs?"

Pat began to feel very stressful and mistrustful of the army men. She tried not to say anything more, but Mr. Donaldson kept badgering her, "Where are your souvenirs?"

"I cried," Pat said, "and told him they were mine and why did he want them? I said they were in my cigar box under my bed. I wouldn't give them the box, but my sister went and got it for them."

When they took the cigar box, which contained Pat's "green healer rock," it was put into one of the metal boxes by the men dressed in the white protective suits.

"I saw my grandmother sitting on my bed with the little kids, and she was crying," Pat recalled. "I asked her if the army men were going to hurt the little boy."

"Oh, Patty," the grandmother said, "there is no little boy."

"I told her there was, too, because I sat with him and did things. She just cried some more. And then Mr. Donaldson showed me the triple-TV thing and

24

tried to convince me that I had seen something like it, a robot, and not a little boy. I got real mad and told him, 'I saw a real little boy and not a robot."

"Well, Pat," he said then, maybe you just had a dream about the little boy. Was he in your dream?"

"I didn't dream him," Pat insisted, "he was real."

"Pat," the man continued, "it was a dream, a kind of dream that just seems real. You did not see a real little boy because there are no such things."

"Yes, I did," Pat said, "and he came in the orange ball and looked in my window and filmed me with his eyes."

"Did the dream frighten you?" Mr. Donaldson asked.

"It wasn't a dream," Pat said stubbornly, "and I was only scared a little bit because he looked so different from me, because he was skinny and gray, but I knew he wouldn't hurt me."

Pat remembered almost nothing else after the interrogation, although the military people were present for several days. "After the army men left," she recalled, "my whole family seemed sad, kind of in a daze, and I had no memory of anything after that. We moved to town before my twelfth birthday in August 1955."

It wasn't until 1986 that the memories of the aliens and the military came back. Pat does not want any personal publicity because of these events, but she has asked me to include the actual location and date of this event–Floyd's Knob, Indiana, in 1954–in the hope that there may be readers from that area who remember seeing the military vehicles that came into the town and who can thus provide some outside verification of the things she and her brother and sister have recalled.

I asked if any other unusual events had occurred since then, knowing from my research that most abductees have reported multiple experiences in their lives. Pat, it turns out, was no exception.

In the fall of 1962, making a trip to Kentucky with a friend, Pat got lost for a while before spotting a sign for Ft. Knox. Laughing about the confusion, they retraced the route in search of their destination. But instead, they ended up in a deserted train yard, sitting in the car with the engine off. Pat said they felt as if they'd just "come out" of some unremembered experience, with no idea why the car was stopped. They never found their destination and finally gave up, returning home at dark.

But later in a dream Pat recalled being out of the car with her friend beside her. She saw a ripple of golden light like an "elevator" moving up at an angle and "angels" on each side. She said they were "respectful" of a blond man who seemed to her like Jesus. Her friend was screaming hysterically, "They want you!"

Pat replied, "Don't be afraid, it's okay." She went up to the blond man who was surrounded by a beautiful light. He talked to her about becoming a mother and about a "seed of life." He said he had the power of all seed in his hand. At the end of the experience, he held out his hand to her and showed her a seed, telling her it was for her benefit and to have no fear.

A few months later, Pat, who was now pregnant, moved to Florida. She remembers telling her husband that the baby would be a boy, but that it wouldn't be viable. "I'm going to have it but not keep it," she told him, unable to explain how she knew this. For the next several months she and her two children lived in a garage apartment. One night, Pat came to consciousness just as she was walking into the apartment as if she had been outside, although she didn't recall being there. She felt an odd, pleasant vibratory sensation and remembered thinking, *They came and got me.*

Nothing more seems to have happened at this time, and Pat continued to have her prenatal checkups which showed that everything was progressing fine with the baby. But then in the eighth month, the doctor could not find a fetal heartbeat. And when she delivered at full-term in May, the baby boy was stillborn. The foreknowledge proved true.

Later that same year, Pat remembers finding herself in a quiet room, surrounded by Grays and waiting for something. The Gray she thought of as her "friend" appeared in the doorway, showing her a baby. He told her that she had a choice to see the baby.

"No," Pat replied, "it's okay, it's fine. You'll take better care of it than I could." But in that brief glimpse, she saw a tiny, skinny baby with blue, slanted eyes. She felt that somehow this baby was a repository for the soul of the child who had died at birth, and she said she felt trusting and thankful toward her friend for showing her that the little boy had, in a sense, survived.

Of the memories which have surfaced in the past several years, none raises more questions than the "cocoon people." "I can't remember when the actual event might have occurred," Pat told me. "All I recall is being in a large room with soft white lighting, and one of the Grays was there. I vaguely recall seeing a human male there, but not what he was doing."

Part of the large room was filled with what looked to be sarcophagus-like boxes, and in these boxes were human forms. "They were alive," Pat recalled, "but not animated. There was white misty stuff all over them, and I knew the misty stuff kept them alive. I knew they were waiting to come to life in the future."

The being asked Pat, *Do you want to see yours?*

Pat said, "Yes," and was shown a human female body in one of the containers. "Don't ask how I knew it was female," she continued, "I just felt it. I saw a little bit of human face through the mist, like a nose mouth, eyes, definitely human. I knew this was connected with the 1954 visit, because I remembered they told me they were making a 'new me.' I felt this cocoon was the new me. I felt that they are waiting for the resurrection," she said, "or reanimation, and we will all be able to see and talk with them here on earth. If I were to die now, I believe that my 'other body' will house my soul when Jesus says it is time, and I, too, will come back. If I live through all the destruction (to come) into the new world, I will still need my other body, as this one I have will die anyway."

In her mid-forties, Pat had another experience with the beings, and this time she recalled being in a room lit with a golden glow. She was taken to a desk-sized device in the top of which were circular openings. In each opening was a different colored vibrating light, and she was told to put her hands in the lights. As she did, she heard the most beautiful sounds she had ever heard. Each light made a different sound.

That is the sound of your soul, the Gray told her.

Pat understood that this had something to do with the inanimate human bodies she had been shown, bodies which didn't have a "soul power" activating them.

In 1987, Pat had another possible experience–much more typical of the usual abduction reports– which included her young grandson. "Was this a dream?" she mused when relating it to me. "I have no proof. I was in my daughter's house, and it was nighttime. I seemed to be floating to my grandson's room. I took his hand, and we floated together, upright, about six inches off the floor. We floated out the front door, out to the driveway, and stopped while the gate swung open to the road. There were about ten or fifteen beings across the road in the woods. They all rose up out of the woods at the same time. I could hear my grandson think, *Mamaw, can I play with those kids?*

"I thought back to him, *No, honey, these are special kids, they don't play like regular kids*. We floated down the road to the cul-de-sac. There in the dead-end circle was a ship with red 'blips' that went around it, a saucer. There was a 'door' with light. We floated up a ramp, and I saw my 'being friend' and then I don't remember any more. Anyway, my grandson and I went together on this trip. Or I'd rather call it a dream–I'm not sure."

Pat had a number of intensely affecting experiences that occurred while she was in a meditative or dream state, and so she has been unable to feel confident that they were "real." In some of these dream-events she has seen a variety of flying craft; she has had apparent out-of-body experiences;

and she has received telepathic communications.

One such event in October 1992 seemed related to some of her previous experiences. "I dreamed someone was talking to me mentally," she said, "telling me things. I couldn't grasp the exact words, but I heard one sentence like this: *The destruction comes in four quariens*. 'Quarien' is not a word we know, but I took it to mean four parts of some kind. Then I saw what I call a graph. I felt as though I was getting a gentle warning of the 'bad time on earth' like it is very near to happening now."

Such warnings had not only been given to Pat at various times in her life, but they have been part of many abductees' experiences and are indeed one of the most commonly reported events in this phenomenon.

So are unexplained physical marks on abductees' bodies, and here again Pat fits the pattern. In the summer of 1993, Pat discovered an unusual design on her inner wrist, a circle of six dots with a seventh dot in the center. This design, incidentally, was reported in a handful of cases in 1991 and 1992, and it may not be a coincidence that these cases have mostly come from Florida, where Pat lives.

A couple of months after the design appeared, Pat had an experience relating to this circular pattern. "I had a dream August 7, in the middle of the afternoon," she explained. "It was one of those 'naps' that [makes you] 'hit the bed and you're out like a light.' There were voices in my dream that sounded like soft whispers, and I began to listen more closely.

"There was something said about 'being innocent like a child,' and this feeling flooded my whole body and soul. It felt like being in the state of pure innocence without knowing anything about fear, hate, prejudice...a pure, wonderful state of being in love, secure, protected, and 'without sin' as we call it. I saw a scene from my childhood of the town I lived in. It looked like it did way back then. I saw myself, about eleven years old. My feeling in the dream was of great joy.

"Then a voice said to me, *Get up, child, and look to the Nebulous. It can take you there*. And in my dream I got up and unlocked my back door and looked up in a daytime sky and saw a most beautiful circle of lights with one light in the middle, spinning around like marquee lights on a movie house, all spinning in golden color. It was beautiful, and the voice said I could not go now, because in that dream I was pleading to go to the Nebulous now. When he said I couldn't go now, I begged him to let me see it when I was in my conscious mind. He said he would, but I haven't seen it yet. It was like a wondrous thing for another time in my life. But my overall feeling was that I would have died to go to this Nebulous.

"I woke up very groggy, like I was on drugs, and hurried to write it down before I could forget. The nebulous design was the same as the design on my wrist."

Pat felt she understood what "Nebulous" meant, associating it with the lighted circular object she first saw. But "nebulous" is an adjective rather than a noun–"nebula" is the proper form–and thus there is no specific definition for reference other than "cloudy," "lacking form," and "unidentified," according to the dictionary.

Exactly two months later, on October 7, Pat received a related communication while in a conscious state of mind, explaining the "Nebulous." A voice said, *The Nebulous is a code; the code has been broken.* Pat saw a whole Nebulous followed by a broken one. "I could see a jellylike stuff that connected the dots," she described. "I knew that the Nebulous was then something that was in our bodies when we were created. When we were created, we were supposed to have a perfect Nebulous. This gave us personal contact with our Creator. When the Nebulous was broken, by disobedience, we no longer had personal contact with the Creator. We had to adapt to living on our own, thus losing our innocence and pure state of being in human form."

This image reinforces Pat's altered understanding of God and a spiritual plan. Overall, her experiences with the alien entities have, to the best of her conscious recollection, felt very positive. With a strong religious faith, she has accepted them as angels.

"In my abductions," she has said, "I have never gotten a feeling of evil. In fact, I felt most protected while in the presence of the beings. Some people may say that the beings have the power to control what you feel and think at the time of the abduction, which they most certainly do. But I am hanging on to the childlike faith that Jesus tried to teach us and believe that what I felt was true and good. Why would an all-loving God allow little children to be abducted if the beings were evil and meant to do us harm? I don't believe God would allow it. Even so," Pat conceded, "there are things which the beings do that seem wrong to us and seem violent."

There has been one very disturbing experience, however, which occurred on July 24, 1993. It involved not only an alien entity but also what clearly appeared to be two human men and a human environment. In the early morning hours, Pat awoke in a very groggy condition, feeling as if she'd been drugged, and hearing a strange noise very near her, making staccato *psss, pssss, psss, psss* sounds.

Then she remembered. Two men had come into her bedroom, carried her outside and into a waiting vehicle, a large "military-type" truck. She was in a drugged state, merging in and out of consciousness as the truck took off and rode smoothly for forty-five minutes to an hour. In her brief lucid moments, Pat heard the men engaged in low conversation that she couldn't understand. She tried to speak up, but her tongue was thick and unwieldy. When the truck turned left onto a rough surface, Pat came awake again and in the dark night caught only a glimpse of the countryside out of the large, square front windshield.

The truck slowed down and finally stopped with the engine running. Through the window Pat saw they were parked next to a large mound or hillside. Incredibly, she saw a large doorway open outward, and the truck pulled inside, into the hill. The interior was very dimly lit, but as the vehicle stopped inside, Pat saw a strange being standing as if waiting for their arrival. The being was no more than three feet tall, dressed in a black hooded cape.

Looking at the being groggily, Pat thought, *What is an oriental girl doing here?*

And immediately a telepathic message came back from the being, *I know you don't like me.*

No, Pat thought, *no, I don't. I don't want to do this again. But they can't break me, because they couldn't do it before.*

When the truck parked and she was assisted out, stepping a long way down from the high passenger compartment, Pat saw that the area was crowded and "dirty" feeling, with boxes and "junk" stacked along one wall. In the middle of the large room was a stainless steel table, more human-looking than the tables she remembered from alien encounters, and she felt very uneasy.

"They wanted me to get on it," she said, "but I didn't want to. Not that table." But she did get on it, although she didn't remember much about what may have happened. The "oriental girl" hovered around her, moving close and poking at her with some object Pat couldn't see. But she did see the entity's face close to hers, its skin a greenish-gray color. When the creature's eyes blinked and its lids met in the middle, Pat said the effect was repugnant, reminding her of a lizard.

Her next recollection was of getting down from the table and trying to see what the "oriental girl" was doing to her. The entity kept moving around Pat, much to her irritation, making an erratic *psss, pssss, psss* sound. Trying to support herself by holding to the table, she moved away from the entity, but it continued to poke at her. Pat was more alert but still unsteady, and as she circled the table she stubbed her toe painfully against it. Looking down at her foot, she noticed in surprise that the floor was covered with sawdust. *God*, she thought, *this isn't even a real floor!*

With a bit more awareness, Pat avoided the being as much as she could, feeling that whatever it was doing was a sort of "torment." Suddenly she blacked out, and when she came back to consciousness, in her bed, the *psss, pssss* was audible there beside her briefly.

Two days later, Pat noticed a slight bruise on her wrist, with a red dot or puncture inside it. And she also saw that one of her toenails was badly chipped, almost into the quick, as if it had forcefully struck something hard.

"I didn't like that situation at all," Pat told me, "and I knew that it wasn't the first time I had seen that 'oriental girl.' I've been on that table before, too," she added, remembering how uneasy it made her feel.

She knew that the greenish-skinned, lizard-eyed being was not human, even though the men, the truck, the travel, and the underground facility all certainly seemed to be.

"What kind of aliens," she wondered, "are involved with the government or military?"

III

POLLY

Polly first contacted me in late 1992, before she even finished reading INTO THE FRINGE. "I am on page 176," her letter said, "and I had to stop to write you."

A passage discussing alien interest in human sexuality had struck a chord that resonated with some of her possible experiences. In the small town where she lived, Polly said, she couldn't find a good support system because the only UFO study group in the area had no women. She asked if I could put her in touch with other female abductees "for mutually beneficial correspondence." What she needed to discuss was too intimate for sharing with anyone other than another woman with similar experiences.

"I have been involved with the UFO phenomenon apparently all my life, and my children also are or have been involved," she wrote. "My father also has had experiences, but he is very careful whom he talks to about them, as he is respected as a technical person and is active still in [a military organization]."

Polly explained that she needed "a woman abductee buddy" because of the sexual nature of some of the events she had endured. "I have all my life been seriously traumatized, with the symptoms of a victim of long-term incest," she wrote, noting that her obsession with "fantasies of strange sexual abuse involving [unfamiliar] intrusive instruments" began when she was four years old.

And its consequences had deeply affected her adult life. "You stopped me short with your discussion of alien-instigated sexual obsessions," she continued. "I have since my teen years found myself every few years in a totally irrational sexually obsessive relationship, characterized by some intelligence talking to me in my mind, directing my actions, and apparently setting up bizarre coincidences to stage interactions."

For the most part, Polly noted, her personal relationships had not been obsessive. But having learned from experience that she could be externally manipulated in her sexual activities, she no longer sought out such involvements. "I now simply stay out of all relationships of a sexual nature," she told me. "The sexual and 'psychic' energy in [the last relationship] was intense to the point of being ridiculous, totally 'directed' and involved frequent telepathy and transference of feelings. I am in counseling for childhood incest, but there is only so far I can go with it, because I don't have a human incest background."

Polly's letter listed several UFO sightings and alien-encounter incidents in her family's experiences, and most of the details were familiar from my research with other abductees. The list included "interactions with 'Elves'; a creature that seemed to slosh through physical objects as if they were water; the usual zigzagging lights; lights that appeared outside my window every night at about the same time and watched me for several hours; maddening poltergeist activity; and many, many vivid 'abduction' dreams."

"I make no claim for them," Polly wrote, "but I know how they felt, a sense since young childhood that something was in my head to keep track of me, a squealing sound sort of in my head which seems associated with contact, and bedroom visitors which my dog, my son, and I all saw."

Polly had merely listed these events, but as a researcher I was interested in the details. I was also interested in the person who was trying to cope with this phenomenon. Replying to her letter, I asked for more information about her experiences and offered to be a good listener, both as an abductee and a woman. Although I had no recollection of any sexually oriented encounters myself, I had learned much from others who had been through such events. And my husband Casey, whose full account is related in INTO THE FRINGE, had himself experienced a sexual scenario with what appeared to be a hybrid alien female when he was a very young teen. Such events, I knew, were real in terms of their sensations and aftereffects, and any understanding of these scenarios would shed important light on the overall abduction agenda.

I explained these two concerns when I answered Polly's letter, and she agreed to share her information with me as part of my ongoing research. Through letters, phone calls, and taped discussions, I learned much about Polly and the things she and her children had experienced. A tall, fair, striking woman in her mid-forties, Polly's ethnic background is European, primarily Celtic, and Scandinavian. She is an excellent artist, but much of the time in supporting her family she has worked at rather physical jobs. Polly was born in 1946 in New Jersey and grew up in the Southeast.

Widowed, she now lives with her children in the Adirondacks.

In addition to the various UFO sightings they had witnessed in this area, it soon became clear that her youngest son, Sam, was also having current alien encounters. In his taped communications and the drawings and reports to Polly which were shared with me, Sam showed unusual maturity and insight for an eleven-year-old.

Everything they told me came strictly from their conscious recollections which, concerning any given event, were very incomplete. Polly relegated some of her experiences to the "vivid dream" category, a common response of many abductees. The statement, "I make no claim for them," meant that she could not objectively verify these events as part of our "usual" reality. Some of them are similar to the virtual-reality scenario (VRS) dream discussed earlier, and some seem to have been simply the surfacing memories of actual events. Nonetheless, to Polly they were "experienced" events, and if they occurred strictly within a mental or psychic framework they still gave her every semblance of reality. The nature of that "reality" was often ambiguous, however, but there were some experiences she had verified as "real" because they had been multiply witnessed or perceived while she knew herself to be in a conscious state of mind.

These began very early in Polly's childhood. "When I was four years old," she told me, "I saw the skinny being who appeared in silhouette against my window shade. It was night, but a bright light, perhaps orangish in color, shone from the other side of the shade. The room was dark except for the illumination outside the shaded window. The being turned to approach me. When I get to this point in the memory, I start shaking my head and saying, 'No, no,' and then the memory stops. I tell myself if the memory comes over me again, I will get beyond this point and find out what happens next, but I never do."

This was also the age, probably not coincidentally, at which she began having the sexual fantasies of "intrusive unfamiliar instruments" used on her. Additionally she reported, "About age four, I had a sense of something having been put behind my left ear."

The next event possibly related to alien activity occurred around the age of fourteen: the onset of an obsession with understanding "the workings of the universe." She explained, "It was like I awakened to a sense of cosmic mission and to an apocalyptic sort of sense of human destiny. I felt I must understand the universe. It became a constant undercurrent of striving which persists even now." Given the reports of other abductees, some of which will be presented later, it was interesting that she related this "job and task on earth" to "Armageddon."

When she was in her late twenties, living in a different location, the next event took place. "Outside the cabin in the Blue Ridge Mountains," she said, "very loud stomping, like several men in work boots, suddenly began on our front porch after no sound of approach. We saw shadowy figures accompanying the very loud stomping. But I don't remember it stopping. I recollect we went to sleep in the midst of all this commotion, which of course makes no sense if we were lying only a few yards from prowlers. We awoke in the morning, remembered the stomping and shadowy figures, and went outside to hunt for footprints but found none."

In early 1987, however, Polly had a conscious look at her mysterious intruders. While sick in bed, she said, "I had a couple of bedroom visitations by two black-robed figures. They had large slanted, glowing, lemon-yellow eyes with no pupils, just like lights. The black-robed figures were about four feet tall. They were identical except that one was a little lighter, like charcoal gray instead of black. When they moved they did everything simultaneously to each other. They glided through my son's toy box when they left–the lower parts of their robes just went right through it."

Polly noted that this event occurred before she had ever seen the cover of Whitley Strieber's COMMUNION or any other representation of the typical Gray alien figures.

"Someone asked me if I had asked the figures what they wanted. My response was NO! I didn't want to give them any openers! My feeling was that they had come to take me permanently, and I devoted all my energy to rebuking them."

An extremely unusual series of events commenced in late 1987. "The whole thing started with a dream," Polly explained. "I dreamed I was flying over the Atlantic toward the Mediterranean. A white plane with red markings shaped like a small Concorde was approaching me from the opposite direction, the east.

"Shortly after this dream," Polly continued, "I noticed that I was having conversations in my head in French. This was most apt to happen around 4 p.m. My communicator identified himself as a professor in a Russian university. I had a sense of it being near Kiev. At night he would privately beam out psychic messages toward the West in an effort to expose a situation of psychic warfare which he claimed was being waged between political powers worldwide, and in an effort to help bring about peace between the then-USSR and the West.

"One thing I remember him saying very strongly was *maintenant c'est la guêrre, maintenant c'est la guêrre,* and he emphasized *maintenant,* telling me that psychic warfare was now being waged, directed to influence people in high positions and others who could serve the purposes of the perpetrators—perhaps obscure people who could nevertheless influence events and public opinion."

Her last contact with Evec was in December 1987 as she drove her son, through a snowstorm, to another town. The driving conditions took all her concentration, so she was startled when the French communication began.

"Evec was saying that he wanted me to join with him in prayer for world peace. So I tried praying in French, and that was a total disaster. I don't remember whose idea it was, but we decided to pray in Latin, and that went much better. I was saying things from the Mass in Latin, clearly seeing the snowy surroundings and driving competently, but just as clearly I began to see, like in some sort of parallel vision, the inside of a (probably Russian Orthodox) cathedral. There was a priest in a dark red robe with some kind of tall, funny hat. The interior was not ornate, but the ceiling was high and there was a lot of rich, polished wood. There was a choir consisting of both men and women.

42

"I wish I had had a tape recorder in my head. The choir was singing the most magnificent mass I had ever heard. I could clearly distinguish that it was sometimes in eight-part harmony. It was all in Latin, and it was definitely not any mass that I have sung or heard. This went on for a long time, the whole rest of the ride. I don't recollect it ending, but we did arrive at our destination. This was the last time I ever heard from Evec. I had the feeling we had accomplished all we could together. He had not been seeking me–just 'broadcasting'–he was sending in general, and I happened to pick him up."

These two events in 1987, Polly's visitations by the black-robed beings and the recurrent telepathic conversations with Evec, marked the onset of what would prove to be frequent UFO and alien-related activities in her family's lives. It seemed to focus on Polly and her youngest child, Sam.

A few months after Evec's last communication, Sam had an encounter that paralleled Polly's experience with the black-robed beings. At age six, he saw "black figures flying about the room." Although they were similar to the beings Polly had witnessed, Sam described these characters as "smoke-like" with red eyes. They told him, *Come with us, we'll take you to a better place.*

But Sam wasn't convinced of their good intentions, and even though he was quite young he refused the offer. "No way," he replied, "I'm not going anywhere with you guys!"

After this incident both he and Polly had a number of experiences involving UFO sightings, mainly witnessed from a nearby hill, and a series of the "vivid dream" events that indicated repeated alien encounters.

"We've seen many UFOs with colored lights around them or shooting out from them," she said, reporting that it was "common to see white central lights flash amber, red, and blue."

This was also the onset of several experiences with what Polly and her family referred to as the "Elves." These beings, she said, "would squeak-talk very loud at night" and were extremely frightening to another of her children who also witnessed some of this activity during the most intense period of activity in 1989 and 1990.

Around this same time, in September 1989, Polly's family also had an experience with a different sort of creature. They perceived it as "sloshing" through solid matter, moving "through physical objects as if they were water." In spite of no clear confrontation with this being, Polly felt that it was "reptilian, huge and loud," making "crashing sounds in the woods like some very large two-legged creature lumbering through the woods in a very wet area. This sound had no approach and no departure," she said, "but there was the definite sense that the perpetrator of all this noise was approaching us. This occurred on a night which included a lot of UFO activity. We witnessed UFOs apparently pursued by fighter-reconnaisance at the air base."

Polly, Sam, and others in her family have had a number of UFO sightings, not only from the hill but also from other parts of the area. In June 1993, for instance, while Sam was traveling in a car driven by a family friend, he watched three UFOs cavort in the sky. "Sam saw three bright UFOs," Polly related. "A bright light suddenly appeared high above and a little ahead of them. It moved quickly downward, then disappeared as suddenly as it had appeared. Then a second appeared suddenly with no gradual approach, to the left of where the first one had, then zoomed across the sky to the right and disappeared." Shortly after this, the car turned onto another street, and Sam watched a third light appear suddenly. It flew a short distance and then went out of sight.

Within a matter of a few weeks, Sam had another sighting, this time of three UFOs together. And the following month, after yet another impressive sighting, Sam wrote me himself about what he'd seen on the night of August 19. "Last night was awesome for UFOs," his account began. "I saw one triangle-shaped one which made a whooshing sound for a long time. It looked like it might have been similar to the triangular one sighted in Belgium in 1988 or 1989. We saw it on TV. The one I saw was flying low....I had heard a whooshing noise first."

Another impressive sighting occurred on August 30, in the same area of the previous sighting. Sam said that this one was a large diamond or triangular shape with blinking lights on the front and rear. "It looked to be really high," he said, "but I could still see it good. I could see solid matter inside the light pattern" as the UFO arced across the sky.

Alien contacts continued to occur, usually recalled the morning after the event as both dream-like and yet real. "Sam told me of an abduction dream which he found frightening," Polly wrote in December 1992, "and this is unusual for him, as he is the only one of my children who seems to seek them and even to miss them. It included some interesting disclaimers to usual UFO accounts, such as 'there was gravity, I was not floating.' He said the interior was about ten feet by ten feet, rounded on the outside, but he felt inside there were some corners. He said it was 'spinning and wobbling' and throwing him around. He was frightened and recollected not wanting to enter the craft. He also recollected being able to see out a window of the craft part of the time and could see stars. He said he felt it was 'a blessing' that he was able, briefly, to see out."

Sam also said he sensed having had contact at some point with "bad aliens who are red, not gray," tacitly identifying the ones he had otherwise remembered as Grays, the same sort of figure so many other abductees have reported. Even more disturbing for Sam, however, was a dream he reported to Polly on the night of March 3, 1993.

"Sam just took me aside," Polly wrote, "to tell me about a dream he had last night. He said, 'Can I talk to you in private? It's personal.' He has a partial memory of this dream, or else the dream itself was a fragment. He was with some people approaching the entrance to a UFO. He went through an entry way which led to a place that was all white, but he commented, 'You know how scientists say dogs are colorblind to our colors? I felt like maybe I was colorblind to their (ETs) colors and it wasn't really all white.'

"He said he was in a line with other people and the person in front of him was older than he. This young man proceeded into the craft and approached a long, white tube. He put his penis into the tube. After a little while he apparently withdrew it and left by some way other than the entrance. Sam was next. He did the same thing with the tube as the man before him had done, but his memory ends at this point. He felt this had something to do with the aliens wanting sperm. He said there was no sound and he did not see any aliens. He kept asking me for reassurance, saying, 'That was just a dream, right, Mom?'

"He does not read adult level books and I had never mentioned the sexual intrusions to him. It seems that just in the past year his experiences have become less agreeable to him. Previously he was the one of my children who seemed to feel a need and desire for 'them.' That is not completely gone, but certainly some intrusive elements have been introduced. Damn it, Karla, something is sexually molesting my eleven-year-old boy!"

After pondering on the situation a while, Polly commented, "I think the motive is not sperm gathering, but control. What affects the depths of the human psyche more than issues related to our sexuality? It is a perhaps unadmirable fact that sexual identity is probably the deepest, most primitive, most powerful identity concept that a human being has. Violate sexual identity in a situation where the human is made to believe that he/she is totally powerless, and you have gained a measure of control probably unattainable by any other single act."

Like Polly, I was concerned about Sam's discomfort with this scenario, and its implications. I was also fascinated by his statement that he had not seen any aliens in the experience. Later, Sam expanded this thought on a taped conversation he and Polly sent me. "In UFO dreams," he said, "after I've done what they make me do, they don't let me see them. It's like they make me want to do it, even

47

though I don't want to. I see maybe them disguised as humans, or humans hypnotizing me. I'm not sure if they're humans."

Polly also had a number of abduction or UFO dream-events which felt extremely real to her and sometimes included human-looking figures. Many of the details, some of which will be described below, are amazingly similar to cases I've investigated and which other researchers and abductees have consistently reported. She also occasionally found typical marks on her body, although without any memory of getting them, including "IV-type bruises" on the bend of her arm and "bruises in a triangular pattern" on her upper arm.

Polly's abduction dreams became so frequent and realistic in their details as well as in their effects upon her that in 1991 she began keeping a journal of the dreams and of actual UFO sightings, from which the following excerpts are taken.

"August 31, 1991. I was with a group of people in a light colored room, and aliens were testing us for AIDS. I was found to have some strain of it, but they seemed to be communicating to me that it would not kill me or even seriously harm me. I don't know if this was because of something they did. Others had it as well–many of us were in the same situation. I think communication was telepathic.

"One thing that has characterized my UFO dreams has been an intense feeling of *Wow, this is real! This is the real thing! This is really happening*. Typically I am out of doors and I see a UFO or UFOs in the sky. They land or one hovers above me. When I felt the dizzying sense of spiraling upward [in a previous event she had described], that one was different because I was conscious of being in my bed and being spun and sucked upward into a UFO. I think my mind was sucked out of my body."

Questioning the 'reality' of this dream about AIDS, Polly noted that she had in fact been diagnosed with *lupus erythematosis*, an auto-immune disorder, during her teen years.

"October 19, 1991. I remember a dream of a week or so ago which involved aliens. I recollect exiting a craft with them. I remember flying before we landed. There were other humans on board. Some of us went up front, but on the lower level the underside was clear–not glass but something thick yet perfectly clear. We could see down to a spread-out village below. It was daylight. The landscape below was fairly flat, maybe some low hills off to our left beyond the village. We landed, and I remember that I and others exited the craft with the aliens, whose form was like a very simplified human form–no muscle development evident. I think they may have had on form-fitting suits. They had no hair. I recollect something about some covering which had a seam near where an ear would be, but this is a vague memory. They were quite tall, not the four-foot type."

"October 23, 1991. I dreamed I was holding a baby for the purpose of healing it. He was in a room at the end of a building that was like a nursery. None of the babies' parents were there. I think I dreamed of a lot of stuff happening in this building. I can still mentally see the face of the baby very clearly. I held it on two occasions. It was blond and blue-eyed, a little boy, and could hold himself erect when you picked him up. His eyes were crossed, one worse than the other, and as I held him he started to get a little better. When

I held him the second time, he was strong enough that I could prop him on my hip.

"Then when he was wanting to nurse, I had this really weird thought, sort of apart from the dream, like standing off a little watching the dream. I thought, *What if he isn't really a baby? What if he is really some midget pervert?* I emphasized this last part because it indicates an awareness that we might be interacting with something less human and less innocent than it seemed."

"October 26, 1991. I was in some sort of medical situation in which my head was the object of attention. There were doctors around me. Before my head was the object of attention, I remember sitting up—something about my stomach hurting. I was sitting on something flat, and they were somehow making me travel very fast. I was afraid I would slide off the end and expected them to care, but somehow they did not seem to care. I remember when I sat up I said I could breathe better that way. Then they were going to put long needle-like things in the sides of my head, and I remember thinking in my dream, *When the aliens do this it doesn't hurt; it is just pressure.* Then I started saying over and over again, *I'm in outer space, I'm in outer space,* and they put the long needle things in, and I could sort of hear them going in, like a scraping sound, and feel pressure but no pain.

"The next thing I remember, I was like flying from west to east. I approached a four-corners intersection in the country. I felt like it was just west of [the hill where she and her family often witnessed UFO activity]. It was like they somehow landed me there, at that intersection, and the next thing I remember my eyes opened abruptly and I was in my room. When I woke up I kind of felt different than from a regular dream, like there was something more real about that experience." [It became even more realistic when, in the summer of 1993 Polly came upon that very intersection while out driving. It was a remote, unpopulated area west of the hill.]

"November 17, 1991. Actual sighting, not a dream. Returning at night from the mountains which lie to the east of us, I saw a distant UFO. It changed color from red to white to red, etc., but was not a plane because it hopped around so much in all directions–quick movements."

"December 21, 1991. Had dream of sighting and being abducted by UFO. I was with some young man on a roadway on a hillside. I think there were big evergreens around, and down the hill a bit was an open field.... We went down to about the middle of the field and looked back up the hill. Soon the UFO appeared, larger and larger as it approached us. It glided low over the field and landed very close to us. My left arm was linked through the young man's right arm. I remember feeling, *This is it–like this time it's really coming close*. When it landed right near us, I said to the young man, 'Well, here we go!' Three beings came out of the UFO. They were human-looking, dressed in black or very dark colors, male, and surprisingly, taller than we were. I believe they took hold of us and began taking us to the craft, but it didn't feel real unfriendly. The three were pretty much identical. I don't remember faces. It was like they had one mind."

"January 30, 1992. Had a clear and detailed UFO sighting dream. It was daylight and I was looking east. I saw a UFO which was white and pale blue against blue sky. It hovered in one place for a long time while I and others viewed it. I remember looking at the portholes or windows. Then there was a scene where the UFO beings were among us and were taking all those who loved war and aggressive military attitudes and actions. They were taking even children. I was not among those taken. We were made to leave and we knew that the military-minded would suffer, and we felt really bad for them. I think a lot of the aliens were tall and close to human-looking, but also others were sort of like the Grays but I think lighter. I know some had big eyes."

"February 28, 1992. MAJOR UFO DREAM–felt very real. I was standing with another person or people–may have been first in my car, me driving. I saw them [UFOs] above and got out, pulling over to the left. I think there was one we saw very clearly and two others more distant. There were also planes up there, military looking planes. I remember feeling, *This was so realistic.* We waved our arms to draw attention, and the clearest one began coming nearer. I was thinking, *They are going to take us; how am I going to deal with this?* And then it was like the atmosphere of my mind changed. I was suddenly in a state of mind where I could handle this, not go into some kind of fear-shock at the absolute strangeness of it.

"The UFO was sort of grayish, not all lit, and some aliens approached us, also grayish. They were not human looking. I think there were three, but I especially focused on one who was either sort of leaning forward so that his head was more noticeable than any other part of him, or else I just noticed his head the most. I said something to the effect that we were really going with them, and in my altered state of mind I felt I could do it, but I knew I would be subjected to them in the craft. It was like I knew, but in my altered state, well, I can't turn back now, might as well accept it. After that I don't remember anything. I think I felt a little responsible, like I had involved the people with me in this and maybe it was not good for them. I had a slight bloody nose when I woke up, but think it was related to a cold."

"June 23, 1992. [Recounting an actual event that preceded the dream] my son Sam and I felt compelled to go up on the hill at 10:30 p.m. as there was a glow in the sky which we felt must be from the sun, as it is not much after the longest day in this north country. When we got up there we felt intensely peaceful. Everything was very, very still, although there is often a wind up there when there is none anywhere else. There were a few fireflies. Then I saw a larger, brighter flash of light in the grass across the road from where we sat. I said to Sam, 'Nothing is really happening, but I feel like if we stay any longer it will.' I felt that if we continued to sit there with our minds focused, we would interact with some energy there and something would happen. I felt it had already begun to happen, but that we still had the option of breaking it off and leaving."

They returned home, and that night Polly had a UFO dream. "I was walking or otherwise traveling along a road at night," she described. "I first saw lights, then saw UFOs–round, a little bigger than stars, and not as bright as stars. They were up to my right, quite near the tops of the trees. I said, 'Wow! I'm really seeing them!' Then I looked up. There was one overhead which descended closer and closer to me. I could clearly see the round bottom part, like an opening. I said, with a little fear, 'Okay, take me.'

"At this point I felt a feeling of being lifted which was like no feeling I can adequately describe. It was like being sucked by force, a dizzying, blinding, overwhelming force. While it was happening I felt intensely that the experience was absolutely real, and in most dreams it never occurs to me to pass judgment on the reality of anything. I was sort of afraid, totally caught up in it (literally and figuratively), very aware of the sense that it was real, and feeling, *Well, I'm in it now, so wherever I am going it is not under my control.'* I couldn't see much, but I felt such an incredible feeling of being lifted higher and higher, like it took my mind.

"After the lifting I was aware of being in a white place, but it was not the standard 'round' white room of many UFO reports. I think it was white like white paint, and I recollect a corner, which is also not typical, and some sort of black or dark object. It was like I was seeing only one little part of this place.

"Another thing I recollect was being in some sort of craft and being behind the pilot, who sat on the left side, and noticing his head. It was hairless, apparently with a skull similar to ours, and the skin was white like putty. He turned toward me and appeared to have on some sort of clown mask, although it did not really look like our typical clowns. It had the color orange on it and was otherwise white like plastic. The feeling I got from this pilot was of a detached sort of kindness, not any malevolence but also nothing that could really be called emotion.

"I have some recollection of coming into a base or land while in this craft. It was light, like daylight (whereas I had been abducted in the dark of night). I

54

could see a building, I think with a flat roof, and an outdoor area to my right of the building. I also vaguely recollect at some point desiring to see more clearly and 'them' doing something so that I could, and things came into better focus. In the outdoor area beside the building there were flowers and shrubs and children playing, human children.

"The pilot was still with me when I found myself inside the building. He said they call us something like 'the short round ones' and showed me models of humans between three and four feet tall. These models looked to be made out of hard plastic or something similar and were orange and white. I pointed out to the pilot that I was exactly his height (5'7"). He was thinner built than a human man, maybe a little lighter weight than I, though I am small-boned. A few other aliens were present, also.

"In this building were some human children. Now that I think about it in my waking state, maybe they call us 'the short round ones' because they have so many of our children. Our children, when healthy, are rounder than they. They appeared thin and lightweight, but it was hard to judge because they were clothed. I don't have a clear recollection of their clothing, I think light-colored jumpsuits.

"I felt I was not the only adult human there but that there were more human children present than human adults. Near me was a little blond-headed boy about three years old. I picked him up and held him, and he really seemed to like that. Then I said, 'Where is your mommy?' and he looked sad and didn't say anything. I got the strong feeling that the pilot who stood to my left and others of his kind very much disapproved of my asking that question. Then I noticed a little girl, also blonde. I feel she was eleven years old for some reason, though I think she was more the size of an average nine-year-old. I asked her if she was the boy's sister, and she said no. I had the feeling they had no kin people with them. The little girl also seemed sad, and I remember feeling grateful that 'they' hadn't taken my children from me, but I was sad about these children and the many others.

"There was a big window arched at the end to my right. Outside the window was a little play yard. A dark-haired human woman was tending a group of human children. I felt she was no kin to them, except that they were all human. I did not see the other adults whom I felt were there somewhere.

"I recollect that there was a process of returning me, but I don't remember it in any detail now. I felt that the experience within the piloted craft seemed 'staged' somehow for the benefit of my belief system, but the intense lifting feeling felt somehow necessary and real."

"January 24, 1993. Three nights in a row I have had dreams including UFOs, a craft, and beings. The next night in actual awake reality, I watched UFO activity in the sky, two luminous fiery balls a little bigger than basketballs."

One of Polly's most vivid and recent dream-events she reported to me at length in a letter, complete with drawings of the creatures she remembered seeing.

"On the night of June 27 (1993)," she wrote, "I had dreams which included vivid visual impressions of aliens and appearances of very bright, very real-feeling lights. The aliens did not look like what I would have depicted if you had said, 'Draw a typical alien.' The characteristics were a pronounced brow-ridge, convolutions or folds on the forehead and beside the eyes, eyes back under shelter of the brow-ridge, and gray or gray-green skin. They were proportionately tall and thin. There were at least three and I am pretty sure more, standing closer together than I have drawn them. I am not sure about my depictions of nose and mouth, but nose and mouth were somehow represented. I'm also not sure about details of the lower body.

"I remember being utterly fascinated with their brow folds and the folds beside their black eyes, but not looking directly into those eyes. Also with the texture of their fairly tough skin, which was sort of like an artist's kneaded eraser. I have a recollection of having been very close to the one on your left [in drawing], so close that my face was right up by the right-hand side of the face, looking closely at those folds. Then I recollect being back a little further from them seeing the group standing together, but I don't know what happened first.

"I felt as I awakened that what I retained were two fragments of a much more detailed experience, as if I had sort of mentally photographed those two segments to 'bring back' as souvenirs–yes, it was almost as if they posed for these memories! That is why I could get so close to that one without having to become engulfed by his eyes, and it is why they stood so obligingly in that little group!"

Polly and Sam reported these and a number of other experiences for almost a year, many of which seemed to be reflections or memories of fairly current experiences. And once she felt more comfortable with our relationship, she was able to address the sexual issue and share the painful memories from her childhood.

"The area of my psychology which I feel has been most damaged by 'them' or by some very early influence," she confided, "is the area of my sexual concepts. At approximately age four, I became obsessed with sadomasochistic sexual imagery. The images involved a little girl on a flat table similar to a doctor's exam table, but I think it may have been metallic looking, silver metallic, a little grayer than actual silver. I remember being obsessed with these images day in and day out, and I would try to detach from them by saying that the little girl was not me, but yet at the same time I knew it was.

"Sometimes there would be one 'person' doing things to the little girl and sometimes several. There were generally those who observed. I had the sense of both males and females present. Occasionally a female would do a procedure, but more often a male."

There were machines involved, as well as probes and needles. "The intrusions involved what I now understand to be the genital area, but I did not understand at the time, as well as the rectum. Also, I do recollect needles to the navel, and this now makes sense when I read adult women's accounts of intrusions through the navel. My sense of the 'people,' if it ever was clear, is now indistinct. My early medical history does not include anything like this.

"One thing I did which could have been a cry for help and an attempt to resolve this situation was that I drew pictures of these events. I remember especially at five and six drawing the little girl on the table and the 'people' around her with the intrusive machines. I showed these pictures to my mother, but I have no recollection of her reaction except that I don't think she shamed me.

"If I had been molested by adult family members I don't think I would have had images of an exam table and needles associated with machinery, especially at ages three and four. I think these images had to have come from some source outside my own imagination. This early influence imprinted my sexuality with the dynamics of sadomasochism. I feel this imprinting set me up to be victimized and set me up to expect all sexual encounters to involve humiliation by a dominator."

In fact, she said, whenever she found herself in 'power-sex' situations, "There was a voice that would talk to me and say, *Everything is right on schedule. Everything is going as planned.* But the plan did not prove benevolent toward me!"

The overall discernible effects of all their experiences on Polly and Sam, to this point, are several. Sam has an overly mature outlook for his age, evincing an interest in questions of cosmic importance including reincarnation and the history of the human race. And, after the sperm-taking scenario, he is also, according to Polly, very uncomfortable with the idea of alien intrusions upon his developing sexuality. For Polly, too, the sexual aspects of her life have been altered by these events. She avoids sexual involvements now, in an attempt to regain control over the compulsions that have caused many problems for her in the past.

She has no explanation for the alien intrusions into her family's life, only a strong sense that this involvement has been with her for a very long time.

59

Most of it has been unseen. In addition, or as part of the UFO events, Polly has experienced internal communications from "spirits," although she cannot identify them more specifically.

"They so often enter or I enter them in a sense," she explained, "in a sense in which we each or all allow each other to be there simultaneously. I don't know if this is a UFO thing, but they are multidimensionals."

Her experiences comprise many elements: UFO sightings, entity encounters, dream-events, physical effects, spiritual teachings, and a sense of an unknown mission she must perform. In their experiences, Polly and Sam have both felt positive and negative presences, fellowship and fright, which makes it hard to place all of the events into a single framework, the acts of a single group. There is also the question of human involvement, since both of them report encounters with humanoid figures that have not yet been clearly discerned or identified.

The amassed data from reports like Polly's show that the abduction agenda is much too complex for any of the current explanations, both in the events and in their effects on the individuals involved. Certainly on the individual level, the phenomenon is profoundly disturbing and transforming, but it is even more so when the massive numbers of people having abductions is considered. The agenda, given this level of pervasiveness, must involve much more than the transformation of the individual. The entire society is beginning to feel its effects, and there would seem, from the testimony of witnesses like Polly and the other women in this project, to be much more yet to come.

IV

LISA

Whereas the accounts from Polly and Pat contain several elements that may not be familiar to most students of the abduction phenomenon, Lisa's experiences are much more "typical," in one sense, comprising many recurrent details–although, as these accounts are meant to show, the accepted definition of the "typical" abduction is woefully inadequate.

A thirty-five-year-old wife and mother of two children, Lisa and her husband Neal have lived in southern Alabama for the past fifteen years. Her medium build and thick brown hair reflect her ancestry of Italian and Scotch-Irish. To all outward appearances, Lisa's life seems quite normal. While her husband works at a good job in heavy industry, Lisa takes care of her home and children, involved in the usual activities of a family with teenagers, and she enjoys gardening as well as more strenuous outdoor activity.

I met Lisa and Neal while I was in Florida to give a presentation on abduction research. Several of the local UFO group's members invited me to one of their homes for a more informal and intimate discussion, and when I described a few of the less well-known events some abductees have reported, Lisa suddenly became very interested. We spoke privately, and she told me that some of the things I had just discussed were familiar to her, from her own experiences. Lisa had some conscious memories of encounters with the typical Grays, as well as missing-time episodes, multiple-witnessed UFO sightings, unexplained body marks, telepathic communications from unseen sources, and many dream-memories of ambiguous reality–except in those instances where other evidence pointed to an actual event.

While the details of Lisa's life-long involvement are certainly very typical, the alien intrusions are clearly more intense and frequent than in many such cases. Equally intense are her emotional reactions to these encounters and her need for help in coping with them.

"Meeting other abductees has helped me feel not so isolated," she wrote me shortly after that first meeting, "but my depression is still severe. I can't believe I have them [alien interactions] so frequently. If they're trying to wear me down, they've about succeeded. The flashbacks just don't yet make sense, or maybe they have no intentions to. I'm starting to have military flashbacks, and my phone clicks and goes crazy. The 'Morse code' and humming in my ear has literally driven me up the wall.... I don't want to be used for experiments or reproductions, but how do I stop them? I pray until sometimes I'm prayed out. Why won't God help? By the way, I don't feel special or chosen like they said."

I began my investigation with Lisa by asking about any unusual childhood events. Her responses showed a pattern of activity going back as far as she can remember. "The sounds of things walking through the house," she said, "have been going on since I was small. The shadows [dimly discernible

62

figures] happened more in my later life, from twenty years old on. Like I said, they do it [appear] right in front of me." She also recalled episodes of missing time in childhood. "I would go to the woods–we owned twenty-five acres when I was a child–and come back, and it would be dark."

And the missing-time experiences still occur. "Now, I'll look at the clock and roll over and look at it again, and sometimes it will be an hour later and other times four hours," she explained, "and I could swear it hadn't been but a few minutes. It makes me disoriented after I realize there's been some missing time. It's hard to go on when something robs you of your life, and you have no memory of it.

"The Grays appeared about three or four years ago," she continued. "Before that, I didn't know what was causing these things, but the shadows I've seen forever, seems like."

In 1980, however, Lisa did see something very different from the shadows, in a terrifying event. "A being appeared to me," she recalled, "when I was a couple of weeks pregnant. We had just got into bed and Neal already seemed 'out of it,' and the being appeared on the end of the bed, squatting, telling me mentally the child I was carrying was special and it would be a boy. I almost had a fainting spell. I threw the covers over my head as the being was leaping toward me, I believe, and said, 'In Jesus' name, take it away!' It disappeared, and I fell quickly asleep. It was about three feet tall, dark-skinned, leathery looking. I don't remember anything else." The child, incidentally, did turn out to be a boy. Now in his teens, he has proven to be extraordinarily intelligent, with an IQ that tested above 140 when he was seven.

After going through Lisa's early memories, I asked her to fill out a preliminary questionnaire which focused on a number of events most often reported by abductees. A comprehensive comparative chart of the responses to this questionnaire by all eight women is presented on p. 231. Because Lisa's experiences are so very typical, however, many of her responses will be discussed here in some detail, as representative of reports from numerous abductees.

She had already mentioned a couple of these things–the odd phone disturbances, the beeping and humming sounds in her ear–and there were other details, internal and external, which are often part of the alien abduction phenomenon.

For instance, there were sightings of unexplained lights, within the house as well as in the sky. Lisa described "large whitish-yellow lights in the sky that blink out like a light switch and fast-moving streaks of light." She has also witnessed "large and small balls of red or white light bouncing in the house" and blue, orange, and white lights flooding in through the windows from craft outside. A couple of passages from her journal show some of these typical events:

"August 10, 1993. When I got ready to go to sleep at 11:30 or so, my cat noticed it, then I did–a small ball of light bouncing through the room. It was just zipping around. I probably saw it for fifteen seconds, then it went out of the room. In the morning my eyes were burning and irritated."

"August 24, 1993. Woke at 1 a.m., felt something was happening, looked around the room, fell back asleep. Woke up at 4:25 a.m. with white lights turning, like strobe lights, outside of my bedroom window. Before I could race to the window, it was gone. My eyelids were very swollen in the morning, and also my back hurts."

"March 27, 1993. Felt uneasy, like having a nightmare, struggling and thrashing about, and then feeling sort of paralyzed. I felt the need to scream and resist, and I yelled, 'No!' two or three times. Trying to wake Neal up, I grabbed onto him. I was being lifted off the bed by a force, but I struggled and somehow broke out of it. When I looked around the room, a reddish-orange light flashed in the house and then went to the side and it seemed white. This was about 1:00 to 1:20 a.m."

Another common report involves bizarre, unexplained behavior of electrical equipment in the abductee's environment, and, as an excerpt from Lisa's journal shows, this has also frequently occurred with her and Neal.

"At about 3 a.m. my husband and I were waked up by the radio going crazy, the front porch light blinking, and the touch-light lamp in the living room on bright." Even the phone began to act oddly, ringing and crackling incessantly with no one on the other end of the line. "Finally we just had to unplug the phone," her journal noted. "I was scared."

This was not an isolated event, as other entries in her journal show: "May 10, 1993. About midnight or so, the kids' radio came on and the lamp in the living room came on twice. Neal and I had disturbed sleep."

Unexplained activity of helicopters over the home, following, as it does so often after UFO activity, shows up in Lisa's case. For her, it began in early 1993, as her journal notes.

"March 15, 1993. About 12:20 or 12:30 a.m. I saw some beautiful blue lights coming down the hallway [through a window from a craft near the house], then somewhere around that time I heard a helicopter over our house by my bedroom window. It stayed for a while, then left. It appeared on the scene moments after the craft was leaving. Couldn't sleep rest of the night."

"May 29, 1993. At 3:30 p.m. my son and I saw a dark helicopter pass over our house."

"September 22, 1993. Helicopters were still flying at 11 p.m. The humming and 'Morse code' were almost deafening again."

"September 23, 1993. Went to bed about 11:30. I 'dreamed' about the Grays telling me how easy it was to get me. Then it changed to a room where there were autopsies going on. Somebody human-sounding was talking, and a woman was lying on a table who had been 'done.' They said some people had a Y-incision and some a straight incision. She was a white woman, probably in her forties. Also, sometime during the night a helicopter was flying close to our house, but I couldn't get up and fell back asleep. So tired in the morning."

Lisa has many of the symptoms typically reported by other abductees, including stress, sleep disruption, depression, a sense of having a job or task to perform, disturbing dreams of massive UFO landings and of widespread disasters.

"I feel they have said they love me and that I was special (yeah, sure), and they say that I will be used for some purpose," Lisa commented. "Probably to tell others about them. I've had dreams telling me to go to isolated places and store food. Can't remember more. I have had small glimpses of catastrophes, just a flash of severe starvation, not enough to remember."

A journal entry from December 1992 records one of the dreams of massive UFO presence which is very commonly reported. "In this dream ," Lisa notes, "I was in the dark with someone, looking at the night sky, and the spaceships were coming in landing. I told someone, 'They're finally coming'."

Among the events of actual abduction scenarios–whether recalled consciously, in flashbacks, or in memories surfacing in dreams–Lisa's experiences include almost every type of reported event. Most women, for instance, have undergone physical, specifically gynecological, examinations while in the hands of the aliens. Lisa's account echoes the usual scenario, beginning with the memory of being "on their spaceship on a small examination table all scrunched up.

"My legs were put as close to my bottom as possible. They had something holding me open while they inserted [something] or did their exam. The table seemed to be at their height. Seems like there were two of them. I remember looking up between my legs and the alien looking back at me. It seemed to be very uncomfortable. I can't remember more after looking at the Gray."

On another occasion, Lisa remembers being less cooperative during an exam, "giving them a hard time about being examined. I remember asking them, 'How would you like me to do this to you?' I don't know what they said...I'm sure they sedated me." The following morning, she suffered from a sore chin and a bruise on the top of her right wrist.

A journal entry from July 1993 shows how disturbed she has felt during some of these examinations. "Had a 'dream' of being on their spaceship in a huge room on a table with the Old One examining me," she noted. "I was fine until he showed me an instrument (I can't remember it now) he was going to use on me. Then I got upset. He placed his hands on my head, and I don't remember anything else."

Lisa also recalls, more than once, being shown alien or "hybrid" babies. An entry from October 1993 states, "I gave birth to a fair-looking baby and called it a star baby. It had real light blue eyes with unusual pupils."

One of the most commonly reported events is that of an alien's face up very close to the abductee's face. Some researchers, taking their cue from abductees' descriptions of this event, call it a "mind-scan," and whatever else this activity does, it certainly seems to control the abductee mentally. Lisa remembers this occurring on several occasions. "The ETs like to put their noses almost on my nose," she explained, "and when they do this I just stare into their eyes. Sometimes that's all I ever see, their eyes, and nothing else that's happening."

Besides being told by the aliens that she is "special" and "chosen," as often happens with others, Lisa has also recalled scenarios of training or instruction. In a November 1993 dream, for example, she was in a brightly lit room talking with some people whose identity she can't recall. They were telling Lisa how she should go about discussing the aliens with other people. "I was being told I needed to learn better how to speak about them," she said.

And she has been given information about the aliens' interest in human genetics, another common communication. Two entries from her journal typify this event.

"August 16, 1993. In one 'dream' Neal and I were raising weird creatures, and another [part] was where they [aliens] were telling me how they have been genetically altering us gradually. I felt like we were their pet project or something."

"August 20, 1993. Woke at 2 a.m. and at 4:53 a.m., got up and went to kitchen for something to eat. Had a 'dream' of an ape or gorilla, whatever you want to call them, sitting on my bed holding my hands, and someone was saying, *They are you and you are them*. Very nauseated in the morning and had sweated very badly last night."

Other, more specific, physical effects have also been reported in Lisa's experiences. In addition to the nausea and eye irritations that she suffered after certain abductions or abduction 'dreams,' Lisa has also found patterns of bruises, and puncture marks that couldn't be accounted for in any mundane way.

She has the well-known scoop marks, for example, one on her lower right leg and another on the upper part of her right arm, which are permanent. Temporary marks, however, are much more commonly reported. In Lisa's case, these have included a triangle of circular bruises on her hip–the triangle pattern shows up more frequently than any other design–scattered bruises on other body parts, such as the bridge of the nose; the bottom, top, and heel of the foot; the wrist; inside the arm very close to the armpit; all around the knee; and on top of the hand.

But bruises aren't the only marks that show up. Like Polly and others, Lisa has found damaged areas in the bend of her elbow and scratches, which she is certain were not accidentally inflicted, in unusual places. After one particular abduction in October 1993, in which she recalled being in a pool of water with the aliens around her before they took her to an examination room, Lisa found a scratch across her lower left jaw, as well as two bruises on the outside of her left knee. And she has had patterns of bruises which are so commonly reported that we have come to refer to them as "clamp marks" because they appear to have been left by either three- or four-fingered hands grasping the upper arms or the thighs very forcefully.

All of these physical effects are very familiar in abduction reports, as are instances of blood found on the abductee's body or bedclothes after an encounter. Lisa, too, has had this occur, in situations where the blood could not be explained as coming from a bloody nose or some other injury.

It is clear, then, that Lisa's abduction situation has involved most of the "typical" scenarios and events, even including episodes where she has been shown how to operate a craft and has been warned about the physical dangers of touching a craft during certain phases of operation.

But she has also experienced several of the less familiar events–less familiar, that is, in terms of abduction research findings which have been made public. Regrettably, much of what abductees have reported has not been publicized, for a number of reasons. In some cases, as with alien-human sexual activity, this may be because so many abductees are unwilling to talk about such intimate things.

In other cases it is the researchers themselves who are reluctant to expose some aspects of the events, fearing they will push the credibility of their audience, especially their desired audience of professionals and academics, too far. Some parts of this phenomenon, they fear, are simply not "politically" acceptable, no matter what the abductees themselves insist they have experienced. Lisa and several other of the women whose experiences are reported in this book, therefore, are to be commended for their courage in discussing these aspects.

The first highly controversial area is that of sexual activity. It is important to remember, when reading the following journal entries, that the aliens have superb "virtual reality" capabilities and that without external verification it is impossible to know if the memory or dream of an encounter reflects an actual event. This is especially important when assessing reports of sexual activity with the aliens, for in some situations people tell of seeing celebrities, religious figures, and even dead acquaintances.

One of the first sexual situations Lisa remembers happened in late 1989, beginning with her conscious awareness of the aliens' presence. Lying in bed, she woke up and saw a group of aliens, one of which held a wand-like instrument, around the bed. The tallest of the beings was touching Neal's chest. "I looked at them," Lisa explained, "and told them not to touch him and to leave him alone. That's the night I got to see them for a few seconds in an unaltered state. Then they pointed the wand at my forehead, made me feel dizzy, and I was out. I believe that's the night they made me have sex while they watched."

The sexual interaction involved another abductee. Lisa said the man gave her his name, T. M. Reiss, which he spelled for her. "He told me they had been abducting him since he was a child," she said. "He was very sorry."

In a couple of the sexual scenarios, Lisa recalled interacting with creatures of some sort. These types of bizarre reports turn up less frequently in the research, but they are not unheard of. She recalled the first episode as a dream-event, in which she and a gorilla-type creature were sexually engaged. Lisa woke up after having this 'dream' when the sound of a "breathing device" brought her to consciousness. She saw a dim figure in the doorway step out of sight and then, as unlikely as such a response always seems in these situations, she went back to sleep. The action, however, was not yet over. At 3:25 she woke up again, flinging her arms about and trying to rouse Neal, who was completely unresponsive. She saw a lighted object outside the bedroom window, and she could feel an energy controlling her body.

"They had some force on me," she said, "stopping me from getting up. When the craft [outside] started to lift up, it broke the force. I ran outside, but I really can't say for sure if I saw something."

On another occasion, while lying down during the day, Lisa dreamed about a number of sexual situations. Something like a small horse was involved, as well as a "dolphin," some Grays, and "a dark, leathery, scaly creature" whose features she couldn't clearly recall. After waking from this dream, Lisa experienced the "humming and Morse code" noise that occasionally plagued her internal hearing.

After a similar 'dream' in which Lisa was placed with several animals in sexual situations while being observed, she awoke the next morning with a bruise on her lower ankle and a tender area on the back of her head, in spite of no consciously recalled injuries to these areas. And immediately following another dream-like sexual episode with what appeared to be a well-known public figure, Lisa awoke in her bed and saw a nebulous form move quickly across the room and disappear. Startled and frightened, it took her a long time to fall back asleep, and in the morning she felt nauseated.

Such things made it hard for her to dismiss all these dream memories as mere figments, yet they were such scant evidence as to give no certainty of the events' reality. Whether they were real or dreams, there is the question of motivation. "I believe sometimes I'm made to dream odd things," Lisa said, "to see my reaction to them." A poignant journal entry reveals how confusing this activity can be, how vulnerable it leaves the abductee. "Dreamed Neal and I made love," she noted. "I hope it was him."

The second controversial area reported by Lisa involves, as with the case of Pat in the previous chapter, the viewing of "new bodies." She told me that her memory of seeing a new body occurred sometime in late 1992. Although she was keeping a journal by that time, which recorded UFO sightings, conscious events, and dreams, both alien-instigated and the normal, self-generated variety, she refused for some reason to include this event in the record.

Lisa recalled lying on a table aboard a craft, with her "new body" beside her. "I got out of my old body," she said, "and stood next to it. I was looking it over, and I even looked at my teeth. The body was perfect, but it had my long hair that I used to have. Somebody said they could make people believe that was me," she continued, "even though it was perfect and with long hair. I wanted so badly to get in it, but I did not. I don't remember who the beings were in the room with me, just being overwhelmed seeing the body. I don't remember how I got back in my old body."

Later, in 1993, Lisa had experienced another dream-event about this situation. "Dreamed of showing my new body to some friends," her journal records, "and reading to them from a special book about humankind. I was reading with some clear instrument like a triangle. Don't remember what I was reading." This scenario of reading a book during an encounter, by the way, is a little-known detail reported in a number of separate cases.

Similar dreams recurred in which she found herself displaying the new body. In one briefly recalled episode she was showing it to her doctor, and in a much more involved dream, Lisa felt as if she had actually died in order to get into the new body, which she then showed to her husband and some other people. There were other details of this dream that suggest it may at the very least have been a screen memory of an actual event. She insisted on keeping her son with her, for example, explaining to her husband that the son "is one of us, like me." Lisa had been told in a past encounter that the aliens were interested only in her and her son, not the entire family.

The encounter in the new body was followed by a more familiar situation, in the exam room. "A doctor and a nurse were giving me an examination," she recalled, "and telling me I had hepatitis. But they were giving me some sort of vaginal exam. I told them to leave me alone, that they weren't my doctors, [but I] don't remember more."

In addition to the sexual encounters and the alleged cloning capabilities of the aliens, a third controversial topic avoided by many researchers focuses on military involvement with aliens and abductees. For Lisa, as is so often the case with abductees, the first memory of a possible encounter with the military surfaced in a dream.

"I was being interrogated by the military," she said, "pushed and made to lie crouched on the ground. In the back were some trucks, and beside them were guys in black uniforms standing watching me. The men asking questions were in regular military clothes. They held me down with the butts of their guns. They told me to give them the knowledge, and they said 'at any cost.' I told them I didn't know what they were talking about, and they just repeated themselves."

Since that dream in August 1993, however, Lisa has had other memories of this particular 'event' come to the surface. The most detailed recollection came as part of a situation which closely fits the definition of the VRS dream discussed earlier. On the night of December 19, 1993, Lisa had several dreams of a very ordinary sort. But in the midst of these regular dreams, she suddenly found herself in a situation and environment that had quite a different 'feel' to it.

"All of a sudden I'm surrounded by military men, some in black clothes and some in green," she noted. "I was being made to walk hurriedly on the grounds of some installation. I don't know how I got there or left. The soldiers were rude to me. I told them to stop pushing on me.

"Then we went into an office of some type that seemed plainly decorated. It looked like white walls and no pictures, and the desk and chair were plain. A man was sitting behind the desk. He was a little heavy and looked slightly balding, but his hair was short. He had on green clothes and no medals or name as I could tell. He started asking me questions, about what I felt on the aliens. It seemed like he was wondering about how to get the public prepared.

"I told him that a lot of the public was already aware, and some would never accept it. I asked him how he could expect that, since we don't all agree on other things. We talked, I believe, a little about religion and politics. I believe there were other people in the room. I probably wasn't allowed to look.

"Then I think they brought me something to drink. I don't remember more. I just know this man looked bewildered and concerned. I believe the alien issue has gotten out of control in his opinion. I expressed to him that I was tired of the game-playing."

For Lisa, then, the abduction phenomenon's parameters include witnessed UFO sightings; conscious perceptions of lights, probes, and aliens in the house; conscious telepathic communications; bizarre external physical reactions from inanimate objects in her environment; conscious perception of missing-time episodes; unexplained physical marks on her body; and a number of virtual-reality/dream scenarios involving both human and alien beings.

In a nutshell, this is an accurate general definition of the phenomenon as reported by numerous abductees. But as the eight representative accounts here demonstrate, the details of that scenario are highly bizarre, variable to an absurd degree from case to case, invariably intrusive, sometimes physically painful, spiritually ambiguous, ingeniously deceptive, and, at every level, deeply disturbing.

Three experiences Lisa has recently reported will make this point very clearly.

The first, which she recalled in a dream state, began inside an unknown facility. "I was on a table," Lisa said, "and it looked like I was being pushed down a hall with bright lights. They [her attendants] were quickly strapping my feet down with straps that looked like velcro. I don't know what these beings that abducted me looked like. Then something was inserted in my left ear, I think. I told them they were killing or hurting my brain, then I blacked out."

In the next remembered scene, something very different was going on, this time involving other humans. "I believe the FBI came to arrest me," Lisa said, "and they called me by my maiden name. One man was really mean to me." Lisa remembered nothing more, but she wondered the next morning if the soreness in her left ear and her throat had anything to do with the memory of the ear probe.

The second experience, which she recorded as a dream, also involved some physical procedure aboard a craft, but it began on a rather exalted level. "I dreamed I was given a heavenly audience," Lisa reported. "I believe it meant that they [aliens] invited me to speak with them, but I don't remember about what." A physical exam followed. "I saw myself on a table in a spaceship and alien beings standing at the end of my feet, telling me or each other that I was an excellent breeder," she recalled. "A reptile-looking creature was getting on top of me, I guess to rape me." After this, she remembered nothing more.

The final experience had a much more conscious element to it than the 'dreams,' in spite of its more 'fantastic' nature. Lisa had gone to bed early on this night and awoke at 1:10 a.m. Preparing to fall asleep again, but still awake, she began to feel a growing sense of some "pressure" which became very intense.

"I looked up at the ceiling over me," Lisa said, "and saw images that looked like vultures or the phoenix bird. There seemed to be two of them...trying to chase each other off. Their eyes glowed green, I believe. Then there appeared a spirit form. It seemed to have white hair and a beard. I started yelling frantically, 'Oh, God, oh, Heavenly Father!' over and over and trying to get myself free from the force. I felt my eyes roll back in my head.

"Then I felt a great pulling, and I'm not sure if I was in spirit form or my body, but very quickly I was in the clouds and sky. I looked down and saw the lights of a town and vapors of the clouds. The spirit took me to a wall or some sort of tunnel, and I was going to be taken in. I don't remember more of what I saw. The next thing I know, I was back in bed and looking at the same birds disappearing. I came out of the odd state I was in and went to the kitchen, I was trembling so bad. The clock said 3:40."

"God help me," Lisa concluded, "whatever I was seeing." The vulture and the phoenix, after all, are very different creatures who embody quite different concepts.

A time loss of two and a half hours occurred that night. And so did a serious injury to Lisa's back. The "great pulling" that took her upwards jerked her with such force that the next day she could hardly walk. The pain continued getting worse, and when she consulted her doctor, she was told that the spinal damage could prove permanent. In this one instance, at least, the event was more than virtual reality.

V

∆NIƬ∆

Anita's experiences, while not so intense or frequent as Lisa's, are probably more akin to what most abductees witness and recall. They include a number of details commonly reported in other cases. But in her situation, typical of these others, conscious memories of events have been less frequent and more moderate in scope. Her attitude similarly reflects this moderate quality, possibly because she's been able to reflect upon her experiences with quiet equanimity.

Born in 1947, Anita has spent most of her life in Texas. Her ancestry is French, Scotch, and Native American. A wife, mother, and grandmother, she is attractive and intelligent. For a while, she was a trained volunteer emergency medic, and later she owned and operated her own business. From her home in a large central Texas city, Anita now takes care of her family and also pursues several intellectual interests. In the past several years, for instance, she has been drawn to a study of psychic and alternative methods of healing. Anita has been consciously aware of UFO activity since childhood, and her brothers and sisters have also had recurrent UFO events throughout their lives. So, perhaps, may have some of Anita's children and grandchildren.

Her first conscious encounter with the unknown was at the age of five. "I recall sitting in my front yard one afternoon," she said, "and sensing someone watching me. I turned around, and back behind me stood a man in a red flight suit. I have no memory of what happened after that."

Like many abductees, what she recalled from childhood was frequently unexplained, but not necessarily related to UFOs. The nature of the events remained ambiguous.

Episodes of missing time which have recurred throughout her life began at an early age. She recalled one such episode that happened at the family home, which was in a very rural setting. "I suddenly came out of what I call 'mind blank'," Anita explained. "I found myself close to a creek near our house. I did not know how I got there. The strangest thing was that I was coatless and shoeless, and it was miserably cold outside."

While these two events in isolation don't necessitate a UFO-based explanation, in the context of Anita's life-long experiences, they prove to be very typical of abduction patterns. And the third consciously remembered event from her childhood did bring UFOs into the picture.

"When I was twelve," Anita reported, "my brother shouted one night for me to come look out the window. I did, and just above tree level, about a quarter of a mile from our house, was a large band of beautiful lights moving from west to east. They appeared to be all on one craft. My brother was around ten at the time. He said it was a UFO. There was no sound, and we had our windows open."

Anita and others in her family have continued to have UFO sightings from time to time. Her older brother, for instance, who is a long-distance truck driver, has reported a number of sightings especially in the southwest part of the country, although elsewhere as well.

"He tells of a time he and his wife had stopped on the highway, somewhere up around Nebraska, to get some sleep," Anita related. "They were awakened by a very bright light shining down on them. They got out to see what it was but couldn't because the light blinded them. They said it didn't make any noise, and that is what frightened them. They jumped back in the truck and headed for Scott's Bluff. Whatever it was followed them all the way."

For Anita, the strange experiences continued into her adulthood. In the 1970s, she lived in Houston for a while, and it was there that a number of events occurred. The most traumatic and terrifying was in 1972, when at age twenty-five, Anita had her second encounter with the man in the red suit. As in the initial meeting, this occurred in the daytime while Anita was conscious, but as in most abductions her state of mind was soon altered as the strangers intruding into her home took control of the situation. She was lying on the living room couch when she became aware of presences there with her, and instantly her mind was clouded. She saw a man who appeared "human looking in every way" bending over her.

"I have never experienced such terror in my life," Anita said. "It was like a dream in that I knew the human was raping my body, but I did not feel anything at all."

The rapist had not come alone. "I could see maybe three others," Anita reported, "standing by the table, but it was like seeing them through frosted glass. I could make out their bodies and the red suits but could not really see any details." She has no idea, therefore, if the other figures were human-looking, like the rapist, or alien. She does remember that after the forced intercourse, the red-suited man spoke to her about something, but the only communication that stayed with her consciously was his statement, *I'll be there to help you.*

Anita doesn't remember what may have happened after that, but as soon as she was aware that the men were gone, she reacted in a very conscious state of mind. "I was so terrified," she said, "that I grabbed my children and got out of the house immediately."

The trauma of the event had disturbing effects on Anita for a very long time. "It is very embarrassing to say this," she confided, "but after that experience I started wearing a tampon twenty-four hours a day so they couldn't do it again. As if that would stop them."

Not long after the assault, Anita experienced a relocation event, presumably with the congruent missing time. At one moment, she was conscious of being in a certain location, and then at the next moment, without any sense of having lost consciousness, Anita found herself returning to awareness and being in a different place.

"I was on my way to the grocery store," she recalled, "and came to a stop sign. There were no other cars in sight in any direction. I started to turn the corner. The next thing I remember is snapping out of 'mind blank' and being [in a different location] on West Road. I looked in my rearview mirror, and there was a car parked on the road that wasn't there when I had stopped at the sign moments before." Although the location was different, she did not notice a time loss.

In 1977, while still living north of the Houston area, Anita had a UFO sighting that was witnessed by one of her friends. "I was outside late one night talking with a friend," she said, "when I glanced up and saw a large orange globe to the north." Her friend, who was in his car, took off in pursuit of the object and reported on his return that he had eventually lost sight of it near a state highway.

It was also during this period that Anita had two other experiences that are frequently reported by abductees. One of these is the presence of small lighted objects in the home, usually near a wall or the ceiling, that seem to function as some sort of remote probe or monitor.

This first event occurred during the middle of the night, when something woke Anita. "Looking around," she recalled, "I saw a multicolored triangle moving against my bedroom wall." She could see that the object had a device or design in its center, where pink, orange, and other colors were moving around.

Her reaction to this strange sight reflects a maddening yet typical response that abductees report in such situations. Instead of reacting with surprise, curiosity, and even consternation, as would a person whose mind was not being controlled, her response was quite passive.

"I thought, *A mandala, how pretty*," she said, "then I just went back to sleep." This is apparently a programmed response that other abductees report, and it has proven usually to precede an encounter. If anything else occurred that night with Anita, however, she had no memory, conscious or dream-like, of further activity.

The other experience was much more physical and less directly tied to alien intrusion. It has been reported, however, to occur following abduction events in a number of other people's situations. Anita developed a rash which seemed to have no mundane cause. It rapidly covered almost her entire body, and the doctor she consulted could not give her an explanation. "It looked like I had snake skin," she described. "It took six weeks to go away."

The pattern of activity in Anita's life thus far had shown occasional intrusions and sightings, but in the late 1980s the activity noticeably began to increase. The timing may not be accidental, as many abductees "woke up" to the fact of their encounters in 1986-88.

Although at the time Anita wasn't aware of the implications, this new phase of her involvement may have been marked by a possible missing-fetus episode in 1985. When she began experiencing some suspicious physical symptoms, she consulted her doctor and was very surprised to discover she was pregnant. Having already raised a family of three children, and considering her age, she decided to terminate it. But the results of the operation proved to be as surprising as the unexpected pregnancy itself.

"I went to have an abortion," she said, "after my Ob-Gyn assured me that I was pregnant. He performed the procedure and said that he could not find any fetal tissue at all. He was as puzzled as I was."

Whether this was one of the by-now familiar procedures of aliens implanting a fetus and then returning to retrieve it from the host mother, Anita has not been able to determine. But since that episode and up until the present, there have been a number of experiences in which the aliens are clearly involved. She has seen them in conscious glimpses and flashbacks, and remembered events in dreams. She has engaged in telepathic communications with some group of entities, at times generated by them and at times by her. And, as usual, there have been peripheral and confirming external evidence in some instances.

Among the types of non-human entities Anita has encountered are the ubiquitous Grays, another group she calls the "Tans," a blue creature, and an off-white creature whose skin she described as "dry and leathery," in addition to the humanoids in the red suits.

Although she is conscious of a single event involving the Grays, Anita came away from the experience with a definite idea about the creature's attitude toward her. "As far as the Grays go," she said, "I have only one memory of an encounter, and it was not pleasant."

In the sketchy recollection, Anita was inside what appeared to be a typical craft. She was being escorted through a corridor, without any sense of the destination or of any preceding scenario. "There was the feeling of dislike on the part of the one [a Gray] who was leading me down the corridor," she recalled. "I mean, he didn't like me or just didn't like humans. It was as if he had a somewhat distasteful function to perform. By the way," she added, "this dude had a short, squatty-looking blue creature with him. I nicknamed him Grimace."

Like so many others in these situations, with no accurate, authoritative explanations or sources to help them understand the aliens and their activities, Anita has had to invent her own terms and phrases. The nickname above is one such example, as is the name "Tan" which she uses for a particular group of entities. Describing these same entities, other abductees have used any number of different names because no one name has yet been established as the proper one.

Anita has recalled several encounters with the Tan group in the past few years. She said that they are very similar in appearance to the creature in the drawing on Whitley Strieber's COMMUNION, which, according to other abductees, is more like what they would call a Gray. But Anita clearly distinguishes between the gray creature that was leading her down the corridor in one encounter, and the Tans, with whom she is more familiar. "When I first saw their picture on the book cover," she said, "I immediately thought, *Hello, little friend.* I know that for some reason I feel protective of them."

Her relationship with the Tans, unlike her one impersonal encounter with the Gray, involves a different degree of intimacy, apparently as part of their deliberate programming of the abductee. "I have never sensed the dislike that I did with the Gray," Anita reported. "[The Tans] seem to be very concerned with making us feel love for them."

But Anita has proven to be quite aware of this psychological manipulation on the aliens' part and has thus been able to see through some of their intentions or motivations.

"I recall one [Tan] looking into my eyes," she described from an encounter, "and making me feel extreme love from him. I put my hands on his face and said, *Too bad it isn't real*, meaning the feeling of love that he was projecting into my soul."

Indeed, in spite of the aliens' intentions to convey such a caring relationship, Anita has continued to suffer much of the same anxiety that other abductees report. "When I said I felt protective towards the little critters," she cautioned, "please believe that it is [a feeling] induced by them. The rest of the time, all I feel is apprehension during the day and dread of going to bed at night."

This anxiety very often causes disruptions of the abductee's sleep patterns, usually occurring nightly at approximately the same time, as happens with Anita. "I do still get scared sometimes," she confessed, "and I still wake up at 3:00 to 3:34 a.m. and huddle under the covers frightened and lie there with my eyes glued to the bedroom door."

This stress response, according to mental health professionals who have studies such situations, shows up in cases where an actual traumatic event has occurred. It may be that abductees continue to wake up at a certain time each night because a traumatic event had occurred previously at that time, as if a preventative warning, a wake-up-and-protect-yourself alarm, is sounding subconsciously.

The ongoing feelings of fear and intrusion are fostered not only by the consciously recalled encounters but also by situations in which external evidence points to unremembered events. For instance, without any conscious memories of a disturbance or problem associated with the area, Anita has a phobia about driving alone along a certain stretch of US Highway 287. There is, however, a possible connection with her alien involvement.

"This [stretch of highway] is where my older brother called us to look out the window one night," she said, "to see a UFO going over at treetop level." And although she remembered nothing further about that night, her phobia about the area is suspicious.

So are the various marks and injuries she has discovered on her body. "Lots of mornings," Anita said, "I have gotten up feeling like someone beat me up in my sleep." This is another common abductee report, waking up with sore, damaged-feeling muscles and joints. "I have waked up with bruises on my arms, shoulders, and legs," she continued, "with no idea where they came from. I have found scratches that I could not remember having gotten the day before."

The evidence for vigorous physical activity during the night, although unremembered, comes from more than just Anita's sore or scarred body, however. In one incident, she woke up in the morning and felt an unfamiliar pain in her right hand. "I sat up in bed," she explained, "and found that sometime during the night my ring had been squashed on my finger." She managed with effort to remove the ring, but neither her husband nor a jeweler could completely restore its original shape.

On another occasion, Anita got out of bed one morning and found the crucifix from her necklace lying on the floor. "It had been on my neck the night before," she said, "and the chain was still on [me]. But the only way to remove the crucifix is to remove the necklace and take it off the chain."

She has also awakened several mornings to discover that something had happened to her clothing, a report frequently echoed by other abductees. In one instance, she woke up with her nightie on backward, although she was certain she had not taken it off, turned it around, and put it back on. And on a different occasion she found that the nightie was not only backward but had also been turned inside-out. In the night during one of these events, she had an altered-state experience in which she recalled a group of Tan aliens observing her as she was "free-falling," an event which did not feel unduly upsetting for some reason.

Anita had quite a severe reaction to another similar event, however, venting much more emotion than the situation seemed to call for. It was in the winter, during the Christmas holidays one night, and she had worn socks to bed for extra warmth. When she woke up the next day and found that one of her socks was missing, Anita became extremely upset and angry at her family. She said she was "very belligerent" toward them, even accused them of playing a practical joke on her, one which didn't strike her as humorous.

Anita was also physically upset that morning, suffering from a violent headache and nausea which caused her to vomit, yet there was no illness to account for the symptoms. Still, she might not have been overly concerned about the vanished sock and her physical problems, if her young granddaughter hadn't made a disturbing comment.

The seven-year-old child told her grandmother that some "mean men" had come in and taken her away during the night. When Anita asked her to describe the "mean men," the little girl called them "the mushroom men."

"What are the mushroom men?" Anita asked, and

her granddaughter then found the book MISSING TIME by Budd Hopkins and pointed to the drawing on the cover.

Anita asked the girl to make a drawing of her own. It showed a long-necked humanoid being with a head shaped like an inverted light bulb. The eyes were black, large, and slanted, the nose had two nostril holes, the mouth was a straight thin line, and the chin was more rounded than in the drawing on the cover of MISSING TIME. The girl said the creatures were about a foot tall, gray-skinned and had four fingers rather than five–a detail not apparent in the cover picture. There were quite a few of these entities present, she said.

Anita remembered nothing strange that night herself, but the physical symptoms, the missing sock, and her granddaughter's story were indicative enough of an intrusive incident to be of great concern. She not only wanted to know what had gone on during the night, but she wanted to know more in general about these beings who had been a part of her life for so long, so she decided to try meditating and sending out messages to the aliens.

"I would ask a question telepathically," Anita explained, "and then lie down on the sofa to drift into twilight sleep, which is really just a deep state of relaxation. I was not asleep or awake. Then the answers to my questions would come."

She remembers, for instance, asking, "Why are you taking human women?"

To insure quality breeding, the answer came back.

"What about when a woman is menstruating?" she inquired, thinking about how she had used a tampon to try to fend off any further rapes in the past.

We know the difference, she was told.

"When are you going to show yourselves?" she questioned further, but the reply was less than specific.

The time is almost right, was all she received.

Anita has used this meditative method for communication several other times. "When I decide to telepath to them," she commented, "I spend a good part of the time berating them for not being honest with the human race. They've always been here. If they had shown themselves all along, no one would fear them. It's the unknown that causes fear. Now they've made it impossible just to be accepted. I know who I'm yelling at," she added, "but I have no idea who, which group, is sending back answers."

And some of those answers have been impossible to understand. In addition to the communications which made some sort of sense—*it only works when the year arrives* and *transmogrify*, for example—Anita has also gotten messages containing unknown words and meaningless phrases, including one puzzling reference to *star planet fill*.

Some of these messages look like nonsense, but one of the other odd communications, *IRU URI*, is very similar to a message given to Lisa, in which she was told by the aliens, referring to some ape-type creatures, *They are you and you are them*. If the capital letters in Anita's communication are written out as words, it would read, "I are you, you are I." And the import of the phrases is clearly similar. Even the grammar is incorrect in both cases.

As with most abductees, Anita cannot explain even to herself just what the aliens are doing with her. And she certainly doesn't accept all the communications and encounters as objectively real.

"I suspect that a lot of these encounters are alien-induced dreams," she commented, "for the purpose of making you feel comfortable with them. As for the controlled free-falling, I think they were creating an enjoyable flying experience for me because I have a horror of flying and it may be necessary in the future to 'fly' with them when the planet tilts in order to save my life."

Her reference to the planet tilting comes from a scenario she has been shown involving future global catastrophe. Such scenarios are so common among abductees that this type of information may well be part of the widespread programming included in the alien agenda, designed to serve some purpose which is not yet clear. And most of the abductees who are told about a coming destruction also report, as does Anita, feeling that they will have a job or task to perform in conjunction with this catastrophe.

"It is like I have always known that these things [UFOs, aliens, and the predicted destruction] are coming," Anita told me, "and that I must try to convince people, and also learn things that would help not only with my own survival afterwards but I must also be able to help other survivors. For instance, I was told as a child, *The children must be protected*."

Anita, then, admits that at least part of the alien programming has had an effect on her, but she doesn't let herself accept everything they tell her or show her.

"I'm always amazed when I get any information from them at all," she said. "I really don't know if someone who would abduct a person could be trusted to give a truthful answer to any question."

She is aware of their possible deceptions, just as she realizes that the aliens are capable of creating unreal scenarios for humans during encounters. This awareness has served Anita well, for it has allowed her to push the alien activity away from her a little, as it were, in order to analyze and assess the events to which she has been subjected. And it also has kept her from jumping to conclusions about some of the things she has remembered.

One recent possible event, for instance, Anita describes as a regular dream, in spite of the presence of UFOs in the scenario.

"I dreamed last night that I was standing in my back yard and looking up into the night sky," she told me. "I saw a rectangular UFO sitting poised about five hundred feet above the house. It had rockets on the side and started firing at a line of trees fairly close to the house. I ran inside, and my doorbell rang."

She said the next segment of the dream involved a scene in which she and I were together, discussing the book project, but after that a very different episode occurred.

"Next," she said, "I was visited by some military sorts who were trying to get me to tell them about the UFOs, and I refused. I kept saying, 'I know nothing, I know nothing'."

Anita dismissed this scenario as a mundane dream, which it may well have been, probably in part because of my presence in one of the segments. What she didn't know, however, was that I in fact had seen a rectangular UFO at very close range in the winter of 1992, so my own curiosity was aroused by her description. Even more interesting was the fact that

94

several other people in this book project–Lisa, Angie, and a member of my family–have reported very similar situations to the military interrogation. And in these other cases, there was reason to believe they were not normal dreams at all.

For Anita, however, the evidence of the dream's reality was not very strong, which is indicative of her tendency not to overreact to possible or actual alien encounters. As a result, she has managed to keep a good sense of mental balance, neither overly exalting the creatures in her mind, making gods of them, nor being overwhelmed by terror as if they were demons. "Not all of the aliens are bad," she believes, which is a reasonable point of view given the cumulative experiences she has had.

Still, when they physically intrude into her normal reality, Anita is not happy about it, as her description of two typical episodes show.

"When I went to bed," she said, "I started feeling apprehensive. I couldn't go to sleep. It got worse as the hours passed. Finally, I turned on the bedside lamp to read. I had not been reading long when I saw a flash of light in the den. I started thinking, *Oh, geez, no*. I told myself that maybe it was the light in one of my aquariums and tried to read some more.

"I started hearing a clicking noise," she continued, "and tried to figure out what it was. Then I saw, in my peripheral vision, a flash of brown go past my door toward the bathroom." The "flash of brown" was recognizable to Anita, and she realized that at least one of the aliens was in the house. She fought to stay alert, hoping to fend off another abduction, but she couldn't do it.

"Finally," she concluded, "in sheer fatigue I gave

up and fell asleep. They really are patient little critters." If anything occurred after that, Anita couldn't recall it. But she awoke with a possible sign that she had indeed been paid a visit. "On Saturday morning," she said, "my knees and legs were in terrible pain. I have been checked for arthritis and don't have it."

Four months later, in December 1993, a similar incident occurred, as fleeting and consciously elusive as the first one. "I woke up around 3:30 a.m.," she told me, "and turned on the television set in the bedroom. This is usually the time I wake up and scan the bedroom for whatever. I turned on Channel Four because they are on all night. I wanted to catch a weather report because we were expecting sleet. Everything was normal until an insurance commercial came on. I was lying on my side and just happened to glance up at the TV.

"At that moment, a black object moved in front of the screen, left to right, and then moved back off, right to left. It had a face, after a fashion, but appeared to be one-dimensional. It was almost as though you could stick your hand through it, but you could not see the TV screen through the blackness. It must have had intelligence, because as soon as I thought, *What the hell is that?* it moved back off the screen. I was fighting to stay awake, as if it wouldn't bother me if I were awake. Shortly thereafter, I felt the old familiar 'zap' through my body, and I was out of it.

"Since that time I have had a sore spot on my spine eight to twelve inches up from my coccyx. I've had everyone check my spine, and they tell me there isn't even a red spot there. However, it [remained] very sore for the past three weeks."

A conscious sight of a strange creature, an unexplained physical effect, and nothing in her memory to connect the two: such events have punctuated her life as they have countless others with alien contact. The alien abductions are something she lives with very quietly, rarely discussing them with others, coping with her fears and uncertainties as best she can on her own. The experiences have changed her views, her habits, and her desires and fears. The whole texture of her life is interwoven with the pattern of an unknown agenda.

VI

BETH

"When I was seven or eight years old," Beth related, "my father gave us permission, my sister and me, to go outside and play with the other children, who were playing hide-and-seek. It was close to six in the evening. I remember that I went to hide between some bushes, and then I heard a sound, somebody else. And as I turned, I saw what I thought at that moment was one of the other kids.

"The next thing I know," she continued, "it was dark, and I was very surprised. When I got home, my father was very mad at me and my mother was very upset. My father told me that they had been calling me and looking for me for hours. But I couldn't understand it," she said. "The place where I was hiding was less than a hundred feet from the front of the house. I was hiding there, and it was daylight, and then the next thing I know it was dark–and I was scared.

"Recently I had another memory about that," she added. "That kid I thought was there, he was an alien, one of the Grays. He took me to a ship, but I don't remember what happened after that."

As I listened to Beth's account of her childhood missing-time episode, I was reminded of a similar event in my husband's past. At age twelve, not much older than Beth had been, Casey and his best friend were playing in a field one day, when several strange children approached them and asked if they wanted to "come see the UFO" that had landed on the other side of the hill. Casey's next conscious memory was of coming back home and complaining to his mother that his nose was very sore and he had a headache.

As did Beth, Casey had a daytime missing-time episode initiated after contact with unknown "children." Beth has never explored this memory hypnotically, but when Casey used regressive hypnosis to delve into the missing time, he retrieved memories of an onboard abduction involving a nasal implant.

This was not the only similarity between Beth's experiences and Casey's. A divorced mother with grown children, Beth had first contacted us, in fact, because another of her encounter memories, involving apparently military personnel, contained very striking and disturbing parallels to an incident described in INTO THE FRINGE.

A mutual acquaintance helped arrange a phone conversation for us, and we got acquainted. Beth was born in 1942 in Puerto Rico and has lived there most of her life, although her heritage also includes ancestors from Spain and Vermont. Beth was a teacher before starting her family, but in recent years she had vision problems which have kept her from working. Currently, she divides her time between Puerto Rico and Florida.

Beth and I discussed her memories of the military encounter at length. But I was also interested to hear about other her other experiences, especially since she lived in Puerto Rico. A great deal of UFO and alien activity has been reported in the past several years, much of it in the area where Beth lived but all over the island as well. In fact, of all the U. S. territory, there may well have been more recent UFO activity in Puerto Rico than anywhere else.

To judge from Beth's account, it has probably been going on for quite a while. In addition to the early missing-time event, she has conscious memories of many other strange experiences from childhood, well back into the 1950s. Her first UFO sighting, for example, occurred only a year or two after the hide-and-seek episode. Beth was walking to the store in the late afternoon, when she looked up and saw a "huge ball of fire" tearing downward through the sky. It disappeared behind a nearby mountain, and Beth assumed that she'd just witnessed a plane crash, although she heard no sound.

She screamed and ran back across the road into the house where excitedly she told her father what she had seen. Since he worked for the U. S. Navy at that time, her father told her he would inquire around the military base and find out what exactly had happened. But a few days later, when Beth brought up the subject again, her father told her that she must never tell anyone about what she had seen or even mention it again. No explanation was given, only a warning, and that made Beth believe some sort of mystery must have been involved.

She was used to mysterious things, even at that young age. "Even before that," she said, "as far back as I can remember, I was aware–and so was my family–that strange things were happening to me, most of them at night. It made me afraid to go to sleep, afraid that someone was going to come for me."

Unexplained noises often broke the silence of the night. Once, for example, Beth was startled awake by a "buzz or whooshing sound" in the room where she was sleeping alone. Frightened, she ran into her sister's room. "They're looking for me," was all she remembered saying, because at that moment her sister suddenly fell into a deep sleep and Beth's body became paralyzed. Then she, too, lost consciousness.

Another anomalous event took place when she ten years old. Beth had been outside for a while and had stopped to eat a piece of fruit. She consciously remembered standing still, taking a bite, and then looking down at a large, bleeding gash in her leg. "I didn't know what to think," Beth said. "How could my leg be cut and bleeding? I had not even moved from that spot." Heedless of the time as children often are, she had no idea if any was missing.

She also didn't know what to think of the shadowy figures that sometimes appeared in the house, although she tended to believe they might be ghosts. On one occasion, though, the figure seemed very real. Beth woke up during the night and found a humanoid figure sitting on her bed. He was wearing a tight white outfit, and he proceeded to talk to her. She couldn't remember, however, any of the things he said, and she couldn't remember his face. Beth told her mother about some of these strange occurrences, and her mother replied that she had sometimes heard Beth in her room at night, apparently talking to someone. But when she tried to get up and check on the girl, her mother said, she was paralyzed.

A little later, at age fourteen, Beth had a second UFO sighting. As she sat studying on the stairs by a window, she glanced out and saw an object through the trees. It stopped for a moment and hovered before shooting off vertically out of sight. Beth learned later that one of their neighbors had also spotted the object.

Even when she moved away from that house, staying for a while after her father's death in a boardinghouse, the unexplained occurrences followed her. One of her roommates there woke her up once, screaming, saying that she'd just seen a weird creature standing beside Beth's bed. The being apparently noticed the roommate looking at it, because it started moving toward her, and that was when she screamed. Her description of the creature matches today's well-known Gray entity.

The odd events seemed to subside as Beth grew to adulthood. She went to college and then began working as a teacher. Nothing notable happened until she was married and pregnant with her second child.

"I remember that I was so afraid that I wasn't pregnant," Beth said, "that it was a tumor, because it [the fetus] was not moving. I told my doctor frequently that it couldn't be a child, that he was mistaken, but it was a big joke to him.

"When I was almost six months into the pregnancy, I was very worried because the baby wasn't moving. One night I remember that I suddenly felt so sleepy that I got in bed, and I had a dream. I saw myself on a doctor's table. A strange doctor put a needle into my navel. When he did this, I felt something like an electric shock, and the baby started moving. I also felt that something was put up my nose. And then I woke up," she concluded. "And when I awoke, I was having a very heavy nosebleed and the baby was moving."

Beth carried the baby to term and it was born

healthy. But a subsequent pregnancy a few years later didn't survive. Beth apparently miscarried one night and isn't sure if she saw any fetal tissue. This occurred, it should be noted, on a night when one of the neighbors reported seeing an unexplained light over Beth's home.

Whatever she may have thought about these numerous, often nebulous events through the years, whoever she might have thought was behind them, in the summer of 1978 an event occurred that left no doubt of its source. On the night of July 17, Beth went to bed around 9 p.m., where she read for an hour and then turned off the bedside lamp planning to go to sleep. In the dark, a light caught her attention through the window, where she saw a glowing object. Concerned, Beth woke up her husband and had him check the area. He came back to bed having found nothing unusual, and they turned out the lamp again to sleep. But the light returned to the yard and shone in through the window. Beth looked up at the light, and the next moment she was aware of being somewhere very different. She was in an unfamiliar round room, and she wasn't alone.

Her husband lay near her, apparently asleep, as was her youngest child nestled in her lap. In a panic, she suddenly thought, *Where are my other children?* A voice from an unseen source then replied, *Don't be afraid, they are here.*

Three other people whom Beth didn't know were also unconscious in the room. She saw a young man and woman, probably in their twenties, and an older man who looked to Beth like an "ex-military" sort.

The whole situation was so unexpected that Beth was too bewildered to react logically, perhaps. Or perhaps, as in other reports, her responses were "directed" for some purpose. At any rate, when she noticed the older man coming to consciousness just as she was regaining her own awareness, Beth inexplicably asked, "What time is it?"

Given the total strangeness of their situation, such a question appears ludicrous, but instead of reacting with surprise or panic, the man simply checked his watch and replied, "Ten after twelve."

Almost two hours had passed since she saw the light for the second time, although to her it seemed as if it had only been a few moments. Looking around, she saw strange, computer-like equipment in the room. And then she noticed some other beings, clearly not human, there with her. The two entities were gray and very skinny, dressed in metallic silver suits.

Beth saw that her husband was starting to come around then. But her attention was caught by a startling change in the metal wall in front of her, as it seemed to transform into glass, like a window. Looking out, she recognized the location as a rural area near some property she owned.

A door opened just then, and a very tall man walked in. He was pale, with dark, short hair that formed a widow's peak in the center of his forehead. His eyes were larger than usual, and his jaw was very square. The man wore the same tight silver outfit as the Grays, but he also had on gloves and a wide belt. In his hands was a small orb that looked to be made of glass, within which many lights were brightly blinking. As the tall man stared at Beth and her family, she got the impression that he was perhaps a scientist, and she felt he was the one "in command."

104

His gaze made her feel like a specimen or a "guinea pig."

"My husband was starting to wake up," Beth said, "and this man put him back to sleep, by holding the glass ball over his head. He did it to me, too, and then I was paralyzed."

Beth was next aware of being back in her bed, with a terrible headache, and then she fell quickly to sleep. Upon waking, she discovered that the night's events had left her in a bad physical state. Besides the pounding headache, she also suffered aches throughout her body, especially in her back, and she was dizzy. Beth was also very nauseated, vomiting repeatedly, as well as plagued with diarrhea. She had difficulty seeing because her eyes were badly swollen and irritated, a condition that bothered her for a long time after this, so much so that she had to wear sunglasses.

A terrible rash persisted for two months, and her hair began to fall out in excessive quantities. Most disturbing of all, however, were the cataracts that began forming in her eyes. Nine months after the abduction, Beth had to undergo cataract-removal surgery, and it was during preparatory exams that the doctor found physical scarring from what he insisted was previous eye surgery. But Beth had never had an operation, at least not by human hands.

Clearly there had been some thing or some activity in that strange environment that caused her numerous afflictions, but Beth could only recall the brief scenario in the round room. She wasn't sure about the tall, dark-haired man, but she was certain that the gray beings were not human.

Not long after this, Beth once again saw one of the

strange creatures. She had been asleep, but the sound of someone calling her name woke her up. She got up and looked out the window, where one of the little beings was looking back at her. Beth remembered that he was holding a metal stick of some sort, but the next instant she found herself back in bed, and the little creature was nowhere to be seen.

UFOs also continued to appear. On Father's Day in 1980, the entire family witnessed one of these events. Out in the yard, two of the children saw it first and called to the others to come look. They arrived in time to see a cloudy-looking object hovering silently about ten feet from the ground with what seemed to be "bubbles" inside, before it disappeared.

Less than a year later, Beth once again had a bedroom visitation by unknown beings. As she prepared to go to bed, she began to feel as if someone were watching her. Turning around, she saw a tall, slender man standing by her bed, and she became very frightened. Beth tried to scream, but no sound came out, so she began to pray silently for help. And then she found that she was moving, going forward toward the man's outstretched hand. Unable to stop, she floated after him toward the window and knew she was about to be taken through it. This panicked her even more, and she feared she would be "ground up like hamburger" by the process.

The actual moment of passing through the window, however, left no impression on her when it happened, and she was next aware of being in a dark place, lying down, surrounded by "a feeling of great speed." Blackness overtook her, and the next apparent moment she was back in bed in the guest room, still unable to move. She could scream, however, which she did, bringing her husband running. But the strange man, of course, had disappeared.

Beth wasn't the only one in her family to witness the alien beings. In 1986, she and her son saw a small white entity. Beth was in bed when she was surprised to hear the sound of water running somewhere. As she got up to check for the source, her son called for her to come outside with him.

"Mommy, look there!" he shouted, and Beth looked, but without her glasses all she could see was an indistinct white object out in the yard. Her son, however, had better vision, and he described seeing a small being by the garage, holding a garden hose through which water was running. As the son watched, he told her, the little being stopped and "floated away."

Later, in 1987, Beth's daughter said that three of the Grays had come during the night and taken her out to an area near the house, into a UFO. She said they talked together in a friendly manner and that one of the aliens even laughed. She also reported the presence of a strange man, who told her he was going to "fix" her heart as he inserted a large needle into her chest. Beth said this occurred at a time when her daughter was awaiting heart surgery.

It was also at this time that Beth recalled having a brief but vivid dream that greatly disturbed her. In this dream, she was on a table, location unknown, with three men standing around her. The terrifying part of the scenario was the single sentence she heard spoken by one of the men: "She is expendable, and we can always use a terminator."

The experience was so unlike the previous

encounters she had remembered that Beth insisted it was just a dream, but the idea and the threat of a "terminator," whatever it might be, haunted her. So did the identity of the men.

Another situation arose during this time that caused her a great deal of concern, even though it seemed to have nothing to do with UFOs or aliens. Several different mornings, when Beth woke up and went into the kitchen for coffee, she found the water jug, normally kept in the refrigerator, and four glasses containing water sitting out on the counter.

The first time this occurred, Beth was annoyed by the inconsiderate act, and she questioned her son and daughter about it. Both of them denied leaving out the water jug or even being in the kitchen after bedtime. The next time she found the dirty glasses and the jug, Beth became angry and found it hard to believe her children's protestations of innocence in the matter.

What were they doing, she wondered, getting up in the middle of the night and inviting in people, visiting with them in secret? Why was it done in secret? Why were they denying doing it? The questions bothered her greatly, yet the children were adamant that they had nothing to do with the intermittent discoveries of the jug and glasses left on the counter by undiscovered persons during the night.

Finally Beth came to believe them, but that made her even more afraid, for it pointed to a scenario of four strangers with free access to her home and family. Yet no one in the family saw any strangers there, and none of the household goods had been stolen. But the scenario of strangers breaking in merely for a sip of water just didn't make any sense. And Beth couldn't believe the visitors were aliens, not if all they seemed to do was pour themselves a drink, leave a mess on the kitchen counter, and then disappear.

Beth worried about this mysterious situation for a long time, even after the visits stopped. And she never caught anyone in the act of entertaining guests or getting out the water jug, which would have explained the whole affair. Much later, however, Beth did have a flashback memory concerning this situation. In a very upsetting scenario, she saw herself opening the door and letting a group of people into the house. She even saw herself pouring the water. Beth didn't recognize any of the people, and the flashback memory didn't show her why she let them in or what they did there after she poured their drinks. She didn't know if the flashback reflected a real event or if it came from her imagination. It certainly felt real, but it seemed so unlikely that Beth just couldn't accept it.

In September 1987, however, an indisputably real event occurred. Another UFO appeared and was witnessed by three members of the family.

"Mommy, there's a UFO up there!" Beth heard her daughter shout on night around 11 p.m. She got up and looked out to see a "huge, beautiful UFO" about half a mile from the house. Her son also saw it briefly.

This sighting seemed no different than previous ones, but it was followed the next day by the onset of activity that would continue for years: overflights of unidentified helicopters. On that first day, an AWAC also flew over, in addition to the black copters, and the craft operated at such low altitudes that sometimes the windows and the entire house were shaken by their force. They returned a week later, and this time Beth even witnessed a craft that looked like a helicopter but flew noiselessly.

She continued to have frightening nocturnal experiences, usually involving fragmented scenarios and time loss. Once after midnight, for example, Beth went through an event of which she only consciously retained three "snapshot-type" memories. The first part began when she was still quite conscious, as she looked out the window at some red and white lights she'd just noticed in the yard. The second scene is of her out in the yard, watching a craft fly away and crying, "Don't leave me." This was followed instantly by her being conscious again and aware that she was back in her bed.

During these years of fairly active alien involvement in her life, Beth had a number of dreams relating to UFOs, the Grays, and other sorts of entities. Some people may think that it is foolish to look for information in dreams, but a close familiarity with the multi-phenomenal context of the abduction situation shows that this is not so.

In abduction research it is generally acknowledged that many times the memories of an alien encounter, suppressed at the time of the event, will surface in any number of ways. It may happen as a sudden flashback during regular consciousness, or it may emerge during the dream state. It also may be that what the person recalled as a dream was not a memory of some past event but instead reflected an event of that particular night, so lightly suppressed that it remained in the consciousness as an altered-state awareness.

110

At any rate, it is wise to pay attention to the dreams of a person with current alien activity. Certain details, often identical, turn up from case to case that differ from the typical archetypal entities and situations found in normal dreams.

This was certainly true for Beth's dreams. In one, for example, she was with an unfamiliar alien being in an environment where the sky was pink, and she recalled seeing an animal similar to a cow. All of these details have been reported by other abductees, sometimes in dreams and sometimes in actual experiences. So has the scenario she recalled from another dream: being given a liquid to drink by the Grays. In a different dream, Beth was made to immerse in "a heavy liquid" and was surprised to find that she could breathe in it. This scenario is so familiar now that it is often included in the list of most frequently reported abduction events.

Beth was concerned and curious about these dreams, as she was about the experiences she recalled consciously. So when the opportunity arose for her to work with a well-known UFO investigator and to undergo regressive hypnosis, Beth decided to do it.

In early 1988 she underwent four separate sessions of hypnosis, all focusing on a single event: the encounter in 1978 when she remembered being in a circular room with her husband, one child, and three strangers. The following account is a composite of the information from those sessions, comprising all the bits and pieces that emerged during the regressions.

Beth recalled that when the light shone in through the window that night, she saw that several aliens were in the room. She was terrified, but one of them calmed her and seemed to be in charge as they led her outside to a craft. The next part of her memory is patchy, for she was in a small room in which the atmosphere seemed "foggy," and she couldn't see much more than several strange instruments on a table. One of them looked somewhat like a hair dryer.

Next, two of the aliens took her down a curved hall through a door, into a different area. It looked to Beth like "a surgery room," and she became afraid they were going to kill her there. She cried out in fear when they placed her on a "floating" table. Overhead she saw a screen upon which her insides were displayed. A third alien in this room engaged in some communication with the two escorts. Beth sensed that he seemed more compassionate than the others. This third entity, holding a black box, then moved to a position behind Beth. She could not see what he did, but she felt as if her head was being "opened" and her brain removed, all without any sensation of pain.

After she felt as if she were "all put back together again," a cold liquid was poured over her head. When this procedure was finished, the aliens stood in front of her, and Beth realized that mentally she was different. Her thoughts and reactions to everything were changed, it seemed, and she was filled with new ideas about God and the unity of all life within that supreme source.

This very spiritual moment was followed by a quite physical exam, as the aliens took samples from her skin and hair. A man with a widow's-peak hairline, similar to the one she'd seen before, entered and made a full examination of her body, including a gynecological procedure.

This was the most upsetting part of the experience for Beth, and she was especially frightened when he produced two long, thin needles and explained that he had to make some "corrections" involving her kidney and ovary. He inserted the needles in the areas of those organs, and Beth felt a warm vibration. The man said this "alignment" was necessary to put her glands in better condition for what they wanted her to do, "in service to humanity." He talked at length about changing the human "vibration."

Next, a young woman, similar in looks to the man, came into the room and proceeded to clean Beth's body with a sponge and liquid. She escorted Beth back to the first room, where the man continued to explain about certain things. For one, he told her that she and other humans were "chosen" to carry out "jobs" in the future. He also described a coming disaster in the world, and he explained to her about working "as a spiritual being" for the good of humanity. The alien said that his group was here to study, collect genetic material, and avert a destructive process which humans had started.

She then recalled nothing more than being back in the round room with her husband. Beth was very shaken by the recovered memories, and she said she had no idea why she was "chosen," as they had told her.

After the regressions, Beth's subconscious became more accessible, because she started having conscious flashbacks of previously unremembered events. In the summer of 1988, while chatting with a friend, Beth suddenly experienced one of these flashbacks. It began with her in a small flying disc, entering a well-lit underground city. The craft flew on through a tunnel passage into an enormous cavern that contained several buildings. Beth also saw some

UFOs parked in various locations and aliens working side by side with human military personnel.

The next scenario is of Beth flying somehow through a body of water, into a tunnel, and then emerging from a lake. She also remembered trying to run away, but a big man grabbed her and said, "We brought you here because we want you to see this" as a huge craft rose out of the water. Beth then got back into the little craft and flew up to the huge one. The entire memory was strange and disturbing, and Beth had no idea when such an event might have occurred.

Shortly after the regressions, in August 1988, Beth received a mysterious phone call from a voice that sounded as if it were coming from a vacuum. An unknown man said, "Elizabeth."

"Yes," Beth replied. "Who are you?"

"We know about your experience," the voice said, "and we know about all the problems and doubts you have, but we can give you proof."

"Who are you?" Beth persisted. "Why are you telling me this?"

"Don't be afraid," the strange voice continued. "We can give you proof. We want to talk to you, so next Thursday go to the botanical garden. Be there at ten. We know you. Don't worry about looking for us. Don't tell anybody, and go there alone."

Everything about the call was suspicious–the use of a disguised voice, the disturbing references to Beth's "experiences," the insistence that she come by herself to the meeting–and she felt the call implied a threat. She told the investigator with whom she was working, but she didn't want to go to the garden. Later, however, Beth changed her mind, so she picked up the investigator and went on to the appointed place. Although neither of them saw any suspicious humans or any alien presences, Beth said a communication about love, faith, friendship, and service was put into her mind there in the garden.

On the drive back home, Beth felt dizzy and ill. Her body didn't seem to "work right," and her sense of time was very disoriented. According to the clock, she even gained time on the return trip, and for a while thereafter, day and night seemed to come and go very quickly. Even more disconcerting was the clear sensation of her hand passing through solid objects as she reached for them. But the bizarre perceptions eventually passed, and there were no further phone calls.

In 1990, two years after the flashback of the underground facility with humans and aliens working together, more of Beth's memories of this event surface in a dream. She saw herself stepping out of an aircraft with two "military men." They were in a desert-like area, reminiscent of the American southwest, with buildings that "matched" the desert environment. A dark, grassy pool of water was near a large metal building that looked like a warehouse inside. An old-fashioned wooden door opened to reveal a very high-tech metal door, through which Beth was taken into a large room. There she saw four big tables and a number of people. Some of them looked to be military, some were clad like scientists, and others appeared to be "regular" people. A uniformed, red-headed man, one of the two who had brought her to the facility, seemed to be "in charge" of her.

Two more men entered the room, wearing outfits Beth described as similar to astronaut's gear. They talked with Beth and the other people, although she didn't remember what was said, and then someone shouted and the group started running toward the back of the large room. The red-haired man grabbed her, and then the flashback ended, but the next morning Beth found bruises in the exact spot where the man had gripped her arm.

The memory felt real, but she had no idea when such a fantastic event might have occurred. Of course, mysterious things had been happening all along and continued to occur–sightings of UFOs and strange lights, episodes of unexplained time gaps, occasional appearances of patterned bruises and punctures on her body–and for most of these events Beth had no explanation or memory, either. It was clear that her conscious recollections about these things were merely the tip of the iceberg, and whatever lay beneath the surface had been deeply suppressed.

Beth might have been able to tell herself that all these events weren't real, that she had imagined them, until an event occurred which proved that the weirdness wasn't only in her mind. In 1992 during a visit to Miami, she and a friend were driving from his house to her daughter's home one night, a trip of thirty to forty-five minutes on the turnpike. They started out at 9:50 p.m. and things proceeded normally at first. But then they both noticed that the others cars, in both directions, had disappeared from view. Beth saw a large, dark, shadowy form looming up ahead of them, which she thought might be a bridge. She reasoned that the bridge's great shadow had somehow blocked their view of the other traffic.

At the very next instant, it seemed, she and her friend felt the car "set back down" on the turnpike.

The driver lost control of the wheel, fighting to steer the car out of danger, and Beth found herself inexplicably unlocking the seat belt, staring out the window, and shouting, "Where are they? Where are they?"

"How do you feel?" her friend asked.

"Confused," she told him. "My hair is standing up, like static electricity, and there's a bad pressure on my neck and my forehead."

Her friend said he was having the same symptoms, too, and that he didn't know what had just happened. Beth noticed the shadowy shape was gone and the traffic was thick all around them. "The bridge must have blocked our view," she told her friend, explaining about the shadowy form.

But her friend, who drove that turnpike regularly, told her there was no bridge at that location. They continued on the drive, bewildered. When they reached her daughter's home, all the lights were out and the place was silent. Beth looked at her watch and was shocked to see that it read 11:55. She knew they should have arrived no later than 10:45, which meant that over an hour was missing. And this time, she hadn't been alone. The mystery was just as great as ever, though, for neither of them remembered anything other than being in the car.

The pattern was always the same: evidence of an odd event, a fragment of a puzzling scenario, and a blank in the place where the details should have been. Every missing hour was a grievous loss to Beth, a dark emptiness in her life. She had seen aliens, and she had seen humans, some of them military, but she had no clue as to what any of them were really doing. The agenda behind these events has remained unknown, and Beth has continued to struggle with her questions and her fears, because the events continue to occur.

In January 1993, for instance, when she was staying in a Miami apartment with her son and daughter, Beth experienced another missing-time episode, and this time she discovered artifactual evidence afterward. The event was preceded by a number of odd but minor occurrences involving each member of the family.

On Wednesday, January 27, they had all gone to bed by midnight. Beth awoke at 4:39 a.m. and went to the bathroom. On her way back to bed, she suddenly felt a compulsion or instruction to go into the kitchen and pull up the window. She became afraid and fought against the urge, but still she walked to the window and opened it without looking out, before returning to her bed.

As she lay down, Beth glanced at the window and thought, *I don't want to see.* She began to turn over to face the other direction, and at that moment she heard something that sounded like a train, followed by the sound of an electronic door closing. Rolling on over, she glanced at the window again—and saw that it was daylight outside. The bedside clock read 6:45. Two hours had disappeared in the time it took her, consciously, to turn over in the bed.

The realization startled her, and Beth got up in great agitation. She went to the kitchen to make coffee and tried to figure out what had happened, but without success. Then she went to take a shower, and that was when she noticed that both of her knees were coated with a chalky white substance, as if she'd been kneeling in the unknown powder. But she couldn't imagine where she might have been, for the substance was unlike anything in her house.

In spite of her agitation, the morning's activities had to go on, so Beth woke up her children to get ready for work. Before he left, her son remarked that something might have happened to him during the night because he'd discovered a puncture on his forearm that he couldn't explain. When they returned in the evening, Beth told them about the events of the previous night: the strange sounds, the missing time, the white substance, and the apparent fact that she must have been out of the house temporarily. But her son, who'd slept at the foot of Beth's bed in a sleeping bag, said he didn't think that was possible.

"She was sitting in bed last night," he told his sister. "She acted afraid, talking to someone. I saw a figure in the doorway," he added, but at the time, he said, he couldn't get up and apparently fell back asleep. Everything about the event remained a mystery.

In this final account from Beth's ongoing experiences, an event occurred which had identical details to a bizarre report I had learned about from a close relative. Beth's parallel story confirmed that it wasn't the imaginings of a single mind. Either the aliens were actually doing these things, activities that were not familiar from other abduction accounts, or they were creating the same virtual-reality scenario for at least two unrelated abductees.

Beth was in Miami when the experience occurred, staying with a friend and sleeping on his couch. One night, she awoke and watched in amazement as "a rectangle of light, like a very thin page of paper" came in through the window. She could see an area in the center where white, pink, and purple lights were moving about.

The rectangle of light stopped in mid-air, and out of its center emerged a full-grown man, very tall, wearing a tight-fitting suit and a small helmet. The man stood up and leaned over her, bringing his face very close to hers. He was above her, but as she stared into his eyes, she said she felt as if she were falling. That's where the memory ended, and Beth was aware of nothing more until she awoke in the morning, in a dazed, groggy condition that persisted throughout the day.

Enduring repeated episodes of such activity, she has no clearer understanding of these events now than at first. She does, however, have feelings about it all, and certain beliefs to which she clings.

Although she is never certain of who has abducted her or what they have done, Beth feels that at least one of her experiences, the 1978 event, involved a benevolent group of aliens. "They brought me an enormous sense of affinity with God," she said, "with the universe, and with love."

But she also recognizes that other forces seem to be a part of the overall phenomenon. "There's a battle of good and evil," she said, explaining her feelings about the situation. "Sometimes they interact in our lives, bring pain and confusion, but I hold onto faith that my good ETs will help us."

She feels very strongly that the future catastrophic events the aliens described will indeed come about, and that she and other abductees will play a vital role at that time. But that doesn't keep her from feeling fear and depression. Most certainly she fears the possible military or human intrusions, unable to forget the threat that she is "expendable."

To face these fears, she relies on her religious beliefs for strength. "My faith has nurtured me," Beth said. "I'm a part of God. Faith, love, and truth will pull us through the enormity of things that are going to happen. That is the spiritual part."

The physical part, unfortunately, continues to include anxiety, sleep disorder, sudden and total energy losses, a number of health problems, and marks on her body that indicate the aliens are interested in more than just her spirit.

Large craft into which Angie was abducted in 1992.

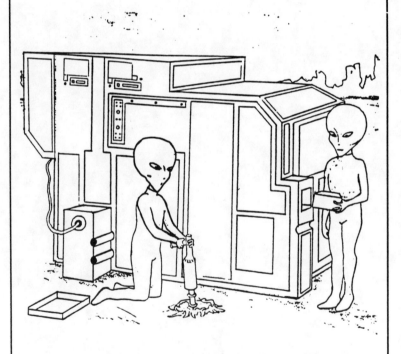

Machine and aliens taking soil samples in Angie's yard.

Aliens showed Angie this 'clone' nursery.

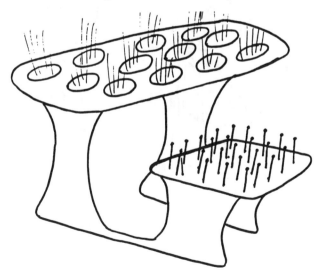

'Soul machine' at which Pat sat and made music by touching different colored light.

Jane saw seven robed entities, one holding a brilliantly lit globe, at a curved table.

Jane's vision of aliens 'activating' certain Texas locations.

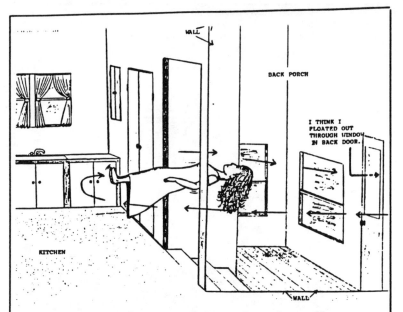

Amy awoke at this point while being floated out of her house in 1981.

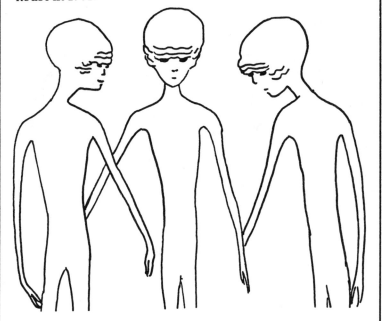

Polly's 'snapshot' memory of wrinkled-brow aliens.

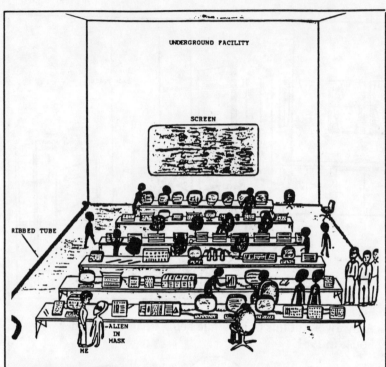

Amy with masked alien in underground facility.

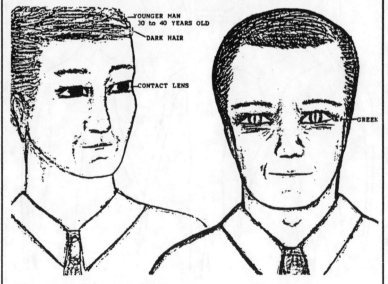

The slit-eyed human figure Amy met with masked alien.

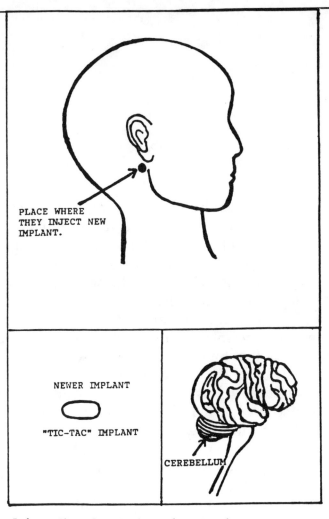

PLACE WHERE
THEY INJECT NEW
IMPLANT.

NEWER IMPLANT

"TIC-TAC" IMPLANT

CEREBELLUM

Information given to Amy about implants.

Ear and neck implants removed from Amy's body.

VII

JANE

Most abductees have always been aware of strange events in their lives: odd lights, unaccountable time gaps, unknown figures in the night, extending back into childhood. They may not have been aware of UFOs and aliens, at least by those terms, but they knew mysterious things had occurred.

In Jane's case, however, her consciously recalled experiences with the unknown didn't begin until 1992. Since that time, she has witnessed almost every typical detail of the abduction situation—a life's worth of experiences in less than two years. And with all the events so recent, her situation offered an excellent opportunity for research. She was eager to share information after our initial contact, and she genuinely wanted to understand this mysterious new puzzle in her life.

Born in 1943, Jane has Irish, English, German, French, Creek, Cherokee, and Apache ancestry. She is a sixth-generation Texan residing in the central hill country. Jane was a nurse for many years, until arthritis prevented her from working, and she has also been a journalist, photographer, and avocational archaeologist. She is divorced, with no children, and lives with several dogs, including her favorite buddy, "XZ," in a rural setting near a large city. Compact, independent, and perky, Jane enjoys sky-watching and music, including voice recitals.

In addition to her professional talents, Jane has also demonstrated psychic abilities. "I was tested for over two years on a regular basis," she reported, "by two research foundations in San Antonio...for psychic abilities." Among them were telepathy, precognition, psychokinesis, remote viewing, and clairvoyance, with the tests showing positive results. And since the UFO activity had started, her psychic senses seemed to have increased.

"Lately my psychic abilities have intensified to the point that it's hard for me to be around groups any length of time," she said, "without feeling mentally 'assaulted and battered'." These abilities may be part of the reason why Jane's flashes of memories have come so often while she has been conscious, rather than only through dreams.

Her UFO involvement began in the summer of 1992 with a multiple-witness sighting, and a number of strange events soon followed. "Something deep and profound has been occurring to me since July '92," she said in our first correspondence. "If you ask me if I've been abducted I have to honestly say I have no absolute memory per se. I can only point to my scars and say I think something has happened but I cannot remember, only flashes of things, and I'm not sure I can trust the flashes."

Like Polly and several others, Jane was not eager to claim abductee status, nor that her experiences would be confirmed as 'absolutely' real by an outside observer. In fact, she made no claims at all about what these events and the alien agenda might be, but she did hope to find answers. And when she realized the possible implications of several events, Jane approached the phenomenon from an investigative point of view. This involved keeping scrupulous journal entries, not only of sightings, flashbacks, dreams, and odd events, but also of her physical and emotional responses to these things. She filed sightings reports with the local MUFON group and hosted several parties of sky watchers on the property. Further, Jane attempted on many occasions to photograph the UFOs, as well as the helicopters and odd planes–sometimes invisible ones, however–which overflew her home.

From these research records and my investigation, the following account emerged, showing the presence of an abduction history. In Jane's case, several things are noteworthy. For one, the frequency of her UFO sightings is well above that of the typical abductee, and several of them were multiply witnessed or photographed. Also, while Jane has not recalled a conscious full-blown encounter, most of her memories have come from conscious flashbacks rather than dreams. Her dreams, by the way, are vivid and frequently recalled, but they seem only occasionally to contain alien-related information, and this is usually in a screened form. Finally, Jane's experiences have involved a number of telepathic communications and sudden "knowings" of messages or information.

She marks the date of her involvement from the August sighting, but for a couple of months before this, Jane sensed something different in her environment. She said she felt as if she were being watched, and thinking in normal terms that the watchers were human, she became very cautious and alert. For a while she resorted to carrying a gun, so certain was she of an unseen presence.

And then she saw the UFO on August 12, 1992, with a witness, and her reality began to shatter.

"Since it was during the Perseid meteor shower and my mom had never seen one," Jane said, "we decided to get up at 4 a.m. at the height of the shower to get a good show. We didn't really see many meteors, but we stayed out even though it was disappointing.

"At about 5:30 I saw a white bright light doing odd maneuvers in the sky overhead. I called Mom's attention to it, and then we watched a spectacular UFO show by first one, then two lights, for about fifteen minutes, until daylight. Mom and I were amazed by what we'd seen and talked about it all day."

The lights were round and white, one brighter than the other, and there was no sound. The first light cavorted constantly, making rapid figure-eight, circular, and L-shaped patterns. When the second, larger light showed up, the two objects raced toward each other. The first one blinked to a stop and the second one circled around it. Then they made a series of fast movements, "like two flies flying in circles around each other." They separated for a while, each engaged in its own aerial maneuvers, until the second object departed to the west. The first object remained in sight, flying in various patterns, until the rising sun obscured its light.

Jane was excited by the event and thought about it frequently for a few days, but then, as she told me, "After a while life took over and it was pushed to the back burner until October 1." Her sister came to visit that evening, and when Jane mentioned that bats had been coming to catch bugs around the outdoor light, they went out to watch them. "It was barely dark, and the bats were active," Jane said, "when we saw a very bright white light coming fast and low toward us from the west. It went directly over without a sound, turned slightly southeast, went a short way, and blinked out. We never saw a shape of any sort attached to the light. And we saw three more lights doing impossible maneuvers that night."

This second sighting of anomalous aerial activity seriously puzzled Jane, and through a magazine article she obtained the phone number for MUFON, Mutual UFO Network. She was put in touch with a local MUFON group and received a form to report her sightings. Shortly afterward, Jane joined the organization and began to read about the subject.

Through the books and articles, she learned not only about UFO sightings but also about the abduction phenomenon. "It was the reading," she said, "that helped me realize that maybe something was happening to me. I had had many of the same odd things happen to me that I was reading about. It wasn't until November 3 that I made a list of the odd things that had happened since July. The list frightened me because it had too many classic signs. And I kept having a gut feeling that something had happened."

One particular item on the list was especially suspicious, as it involved a time gap. Planning to drive into town with her friend Brenda to see some friends perform in a band, Jane left her house just before 7 p.m. on October 30 to make the fifteen-minute drive.

"I was just a short way down the road from my house," Jane described, "when an owl came flying directly at my windshield. I thought it was going to crash into the glass, but at the last minute it just curved smoothly over the top of the car without contact. I had never had that happen and was glad it didn't hit me. I continued on my way and got to Brenda's. She met me at the door, worried and asked if anything was wrong. I said, 'No, why?'

"She said that I was late, and she had called the house and left a message on my phone machine. She was worried because I was usually early, and it was late enough that she thought maybe I'd had a wreck or something. I was really surprised to find out that it was 7:50 p.m. I couldn't account for the time loss because I should have been there by 7:10 or 7:15 at the latest."

The whole thing made no sense, for Jane went back through the trip mentally several times and could not find any reason for the thirty-to-forty-five minute delay, not even a moment out of sequence. "But something didn't feel right," she said. "I think it worked on my subconscious, because it was three days later that I made the list of all the curious things that had been happening since July."

Ten days later, Jane began keeping a daily journal of events. She woke up that morning with a bloody nose, sore throat, and large bruises on her arm for which she couldn't account. She had not been aware of anything unusual, other than a vague sense of some activity. Many of the oddities she'd noted were too ambiguous to give her proof of any abductions or alien involvement in her life. But the UFO sightings were real, that much felt certain, and they continued to recur.

The very next one, in fact, was even preceded by an announcement of sorts. At 3 p.m. on December 1, Jane suddenly received a communication, a very clear message that the UFOs would show up that night for her to photograph. She was given explicit instructions to clean her lens and put new batteries in the camera. "I'll get my camera and they'll show as a sign for me," she noted in her journal, "I feel it strongly."

At 5:30 she prepared, with a pallet, binoculars, the camera, and warm clothing. At 6:40, the UFO appeared. Jane quickly snapped five photos. One of them turned out well, showing a large single light of which the back portion appears wider than the front. It wasn't as good as she hoped, but good enough to make her determined to shoot more photos, since the UFOs seemed to be showing up rather frequently. And after the fulfillment of the telepathic communication's promise, Jane couldn't help but feel that the mysterious phenomenon of lights in the sky wasn't a random occurrence. This seemed to have a connection to her.

The next day, December 2, when she returned home from voice lessons, Jane entered the house and discovered an unrecognizable odor permeating the air. She described it as "acrid, strong, heavy, sharp, pungent, and tangy," unrelated to food or smoke odors, and unlike anything she'd ever smelled. Its source was never located.

That night, Jane witnessed another anomalous light. This one was not in the sky, but rather low to the ground and very close to her house. It was shortly after midnight, and she had turned off the light for the night. "I was lying quietly on my back, thinking,"

Jane said, "and my blinds were open. Shortly, just beyond the trees, I saw a flashing blue light. I saw it at the top of my cedar tree, and then it dropped down to the level of the window cross panes. Dogs all around began barking–mine didn't, they lay asleep–and I thought, *They're here!* My whole body tingled, and my mid-section welled up with something. I watched and didn't see anything else for a few minutes. Then I saw a 'light bulb flash' to the right and then left of the window." Her drawing shows an intermittent light spiraling downward, moving from one side to the other in the window.

Inexplicably–or perhaps not–Jane didn't get up to check on the situation. Instead, she instantly fell asleep. "I was awake one minute–the next, asleep," her journal notes. "I guess I was scared."

Two and a half hours later, at 3:40 a.m. on December 3, Jane woke up. She felt instantly awake and alert, as if she hadn't been asleep at all, and stayed up the rest of the night. Around 6 a.m., Jane happened to look at her back and was surprised to see two fresh scratches on her left shoulder and a scratch and a welt on the left one. She also noticed as the day went on that she was having difficulty discerning right and left directions, something that had never happened to her before. This lasted two weeks, as did an almost total loss of short-term memory.

At 7:15 a.m. the house was shaken and vibrated by the loud noise of a helicopter. It flew toward the south, lingered momentarily by the side of the house, and then continued on. Jane was surprised by the helicopter, because even though there had been an unusual number of them flying over her house since the first UFO sighting, she hadn't seen one in several days. The last one's arrival had coincided with a UFO, she realized, just as this one showed up only hours after the blue light's appearance. She wondered if she were imagining connections that didn't exist, if her increasingly agitated, disoriented, and frightened state of mind was clouding her logic. But the nervous feelings continued, even though she tried to explain them away. "The strobe light scares me because there was no sound," she noted in the journal, "and the light was too close not to hear if it was a plane or 'copter. It was a silent light."

A silent light, preceded by an unknown acrid odor, followed immediately by a sudden loss of consciousness, and in conjunction with unexplained scratches, body marks, and disorientation. All that were missing were the memories.

On the evening of December 4, Jane found another unexplained injury, a quarter-sized bruise on her right hand. Examining the rest of her body, she also noticed a new addition to a pattern of marks which had been showing up on her forearm. They included two circles and two lines in a V-shape, and now there was also a "cut-line" connected to the larger circle as well as a small red dot near the other circle.

The closing lines of her journal entry for that day include a very intriguing final line: "Felt better after I talked to S____ . L____ and I laughed and laughed tonight. I needed it. I feel good, up. I'm not so afraid to see them now. I feel a lot has been connected in my mind."

Two nights later, Jane recorded a curious dream which occurred between 11 p.m. when she went to bed and 1:30 a.m. when she awoke. On the surface, nothing about it seemed related to any of these previous events, but an examination of several details shows a possible screen memory or screened new event.

"A group of women arrived at my house for a 'birthday' party," she noted in the journal. "They seemed familiar but didn't know any of them from 'real life.' They were purposeful and quietly determined. We did some [unremembered] things in a small house. I stayed mostly in the 'bedroom.' I was disagreeable after a while and they were put out with me. One of them I knew better, and she was the leader. They were about as tall as I. I don't remember spoken words. At one point I was real disagreeable and tussled with them. They left me in the bedroom and conferred together in the kitchen.

"Finally they came out and said they had to go. They began to leave as a group, and I felt bad about what I'd done and asked them to reconsider. They said no and looked put-out. They began to leave, and I watched them go sadly and relieved, too. The leader did all the communicating."

Jane enclosed a number of words in quotation marks, as if to suggest that they weren't what they seemed to be, including "birthday," "real life," and "bedroom." Do they suggest that the purpose of the group's visit was not her birthday, that they might be familiar from experiences that weren't part of Jane's normal life, and that the room was not a bedroom?

The group's demeanor is not festive, but rather "purposeful" and quiet. No one speaks but the leader–a curious term for a social visitor. She didn't remember her activities with the group in the bedroom, nor why she was "disagreeable" and resistant. Whatever occurred was clearly not a party game. And finally, her feelings about them when they prepare to depart are strangely ambiguous.

If these visitors, events, and emotions are put into abduction terms, the parallel is obvious: A group of vaguely familiar visitors arrive and interact with a person in a small enclosure. The interactions are disagreeable to the person, who feels resistant. Only one of the group, the leader, communicates with the person. When the visitors leave, the person has confused emotions and cannot recall all the details of the interaction.

Given these parallels, it may well be that Jane's dream images screened an actual alien encounter. Five days later, however, on December 9, she had a conscious perception of unknown visitors. She awoke from a dream around 5:30 a.m. and realized she was hearing "voices and faint music" downstairs in the living room. She listened in surprise, but abruptly the noises ceased.

"Then I could hear someone walking away from the bed toward the stairs and down them," she wrote. "The sound was a loud 'blue jeans rub' between the thighs of a man. I listened for several moments when suddenly I caught the black outline of a man slipping past my window. He had a faint light outlining him. He was tallish and in a hurry. He was just a quick flicker and then gone. I was paralyzed with fear. I tried to reach for my gun, but I couldn't move! I tried so hard, but I was so scared I couldn't move. When I looked at the window, I could move then, and everything was okay."

This intrusion marked the end of a series of events that had begun with the silent blue light near Jane's house. Other possible UFO sightings continued to occur, not always with concomitant odd activity. She watched two nocturnal lights fly in an arched path on January 9, 1993, for instance, and three lights going in opposite directions on April 10.

"The lights would fade in, travel slowly, and then fade out or disappear," she wrote in her journal. "I saw two bright, golden streaking meteors, plus a huge bright flash through the trees southwest of my house. Seemed to be in the woods."

And then on May 16, Jane had a spectacular UFO sighting that was witnessed not only by her mother, who was visiting, but also by several people all around the area of a large lake. That evening, Jane received a phone call from one of the local MUFON members who told her that she'd gotten a report of a triangular UFO near Jane's location. She asked if Jane would go outside and have a look.

Immediately Jane ran out and spotted a light in the sky toward the lake, alternating or rotating with red, green, amber, and white lights. Her mother stepped out and also saw the object, which hovered for about ten minutes before drifting off to the north.

Jane was distracted by her mother for a few minutes, and when she looked back to the west, the light was gone. Disappointed, she stood there a while wishing it would come back so she could make a better observation. Within minutes, unbelievably, the triangular craft reappeared, floating low overhead with a soft humming sound and a *whoosh* of air as it passed. The lights showed different colors this time, with four white lights down its sides, a big white light on the front, and a blinking red light.

As it turned out, there were quite a few witnesses.

133

A local weekly newspaper reported the sighting in its May 20 edition with a front-page story. The UFO was described as "rainbow-colored" and was seen between 9 and 10 p.m. A couple of hours later, the UFO had returned, or perhaps a different craft, because the police started getting reports around midnight of an object with orange, blue, and white lights which appeared to descend or land in a field. Whatever Jane had been seeing, others had seen things, too, and she had no doubt of the UFO's reality.

Nor could she ignore the weird external events and oddities that had been occurring since her first sighting in the summer of 1992. The list of these events reads like a litany of peripheral abduction activity. To begin with, not only did she see the anomalous flying lights, Jane also occasionally witnessed smaller, closer, more personal displays. Sometimes they were nearby in the woods, and sometimes even closer, as in the instance where two bright lights "zipped" between Jane and a friend with her on a sky watch.

Bizarre electrical disturbances recurred, such as a radio suddenly turning itself on, a television turning off, and a broken ceiling light turning on by itself, after five months of not working. Jane also had strange phone activity over these months. She received silent calls and numerous wrong-number calls of a suspicious nature, and her answering machine behaved oddly. Additionally, she noted a number of time discrepancies.

There were many unexplained noises in the house that had not been present before, loud pops, pings, and creaks out of the ordinary, as well as humming and buzzing noises and strange clicking sounds on occasion. Outside of the house, loud helicopters started flying overhead at odd times of the day and night. When Jane reported this activity to the local UFO study group, the pattern changed for a while, and instead of helicopters she witnessed a variety of planes now buzzing the property, including invisible ones.

Several times Jane awoke with her panties inside out, even though she is certain she didn't remove them. Also, she woke up once with her sleeping shirt inside out. And she has found blood on her pillow in addition to in her ear and nose, without any injury to account for these instances.

But there have been injuries at other times, mostly insignificant yet inexplicable in everyday terms. "I've had numerous unexplained odd bruises on my legs and arms," she told me, "and odd scratch whelps on my back. Right this moment, I have a bruise under my right eye that wasn't there yesterday and small round bruises on my right thigh on the inside."

Jane has also had a number of "puncture" marks in various places, including at one point several punctures inside her mouth and on her breast. Sometimes the marks appeared after a suspected encounter or strange dream, but not always, and there were usually only a very few of them at a time. But on one occasion, after a vivid daytime dream of seeing a Gray, Jane found a number of body marks.

"Saw a Gray coming through a door with light behind him," she wrote in her journal. "I wasn't afraid. I was waiting in a dark room. Light behind him obscured his front features. He didn't seem to have elbows. He lifted his left arm and instead of [it bending at the elbow], his arm "S-ed" to lift. No elbow used. His hands were oversized with a covering. Seems like he had a willowy neck. His entire body was willowy, slender, slight, and fragile-looking, grayish color as best as I could see."

Jane remembered no activity in the dream, only seeing the Gray. But that same day she discovered an extraordinary number of new marks all over her body. From her calves to her shoulders, Jane and a friend counted and photographed ten scratches, thirteen bruises, five scraped or scooped areas, two punctures, and an equilateral triangle of three dots. These appear to have been very recent, because eight parallel, claw-like welts on her shoulders faded away during the morning hours.

For Jane, the UFO sightings and the physical marks were hard, believable evidence, things that could be photographed to show that something unusual was going on in her life. She had no photos, however, of the UFOs' occupants nor of whoever or whatever had caused the body marks. What she did have were flashback memories, sudden conscious images of scenes in which she was with aliens. They were brief and incomplete, but tantalizingly evocative of many more unrecalled events.

Once, she suddenly "saw" herself lying on her back, in a dark, dense atmosphere. "Little hands are beneath me," she said, "and I'm moving softly through the air." She felt panicked, unable to respond, and then the memory clicked off. In another, Jane recalled being with four aliens, fighting them as they carried her away, and being told of some impending event.

One sudden memory showed her on a table with four Grays around her, one of them tinkering with a square box to which hoses were attached that ran up to the ceiling. Another scenario involved the aliens taking sample scrapings from her fingernails, which they telepathically explained as a test "to check for pollution."

Two of the flashbacks concerned events in a round room. In the first one, she saw a white, curved desk and a group of seven beings with long hair and white robes seated behind it. The being in the center held a brilliantly lit globe in front of its face, and the features of the other six were indistinct.

The second event, a telepathic communication, came in a flash just after Jane had heard a weird humming noise on her porch. A scene came into her mind, of the inside of a craft which was sparsely furnished and illuminated by a lemony colored light. Three Grays were present, one of whom was dressed in a long robe and another who was busy with control-like equipment on the wall.

Jane began to pick up telepathic communication then, hearing *Activate, activate, activate* repeatedly. This was followed by the names of certain towns and areas in Texas, including the Panhandle, Big Bend, Gonzales, Llano, and the Louisiana-Texas border. While the images continued in her mind, the humming noise on the porch grew louder and followed her inside, where the implanted vision continued. One of the Grays turned as if to look at Jane with an expression of "parental amusement."

Some of her dreams, as noted earlier, seemed to contain scenes and information that could be related to possible alien experiences, although they were usually in screened form. A few of the dreams, about impending disasters and UFOs landing either to

137

invade, monitor, or rescue humans, are common among abductees. Also common are dreams about sickly babies, acts of telekinesis and levitation, and strange people's faces very close to one's own. Jane has had all of these dreams.

Her most impressive UFO dream occurred in the wee hours of December 31, 1992, and, like so many abductees' "dreams," this one proved to be the memory of a very real event. Jane's journal entry for that day began with her noticing a new mark on her body around 8:30 am. It was a straight, "grooved" line over 1-1/2 inches long on top of her shinbone near the ankle. Then she described the dream.

"Had vivid! dream," she noted, "with extraordinary! auditory and clear images, during the night...between 3:00 and 5:15 a.m. I dreamed I was walking outside when an extraordinary buzz-hum began. The sound was loud, riveting, and pervaded through my body, throwing me into a 'void or mental isolation.' The sound seeped into my 'ordinary' consciousness...a powerful sound.

"I looked up, and a huge, gray, metal [saucer-like] spaceship dropped straight down from the clouds on my right," Jane continued. "I sat down on a 'mesa' cross-legged as it sank to earth. As I looked at it, it changed to a sphere on four legs with strange marks on it.

"Shortly thereafter, it lifted straight up and then began a curved flight in front of me and circled to my left. I yelled, 'Hello, hello' and it swooped in to look at me. Its force field was a tremendous, pushing, pressure against my body and was pushing me over, and I started to fall off the mesa.

"I asked it to 'move away, I can't keep my

balance,' and it came right up to my face in front of my eyes. I began to fall. 'Don't let me fall, don't let me fall,' I pleaded. I sensed it caught me, and I lost consciousness and blacked out in my dream!

"I woke up at 5:15 a.m. panting hard. I could still hear that powerful sound. I'll never forget it or the extraordinary sensation. Somehow, I know that that is what they really sound like. The dream seemed real, more real than I want to admit. I've never had a dream like that! Never. So clear and lucid."

Seven months later, Jane decided to undergo regressive hypnosis to explore some of her strange memories and experiences. In the first session she recalled a hitherto-unremembered event from childhood, and in the second session she examined the UFO dream.

Once she was in a trance state, Jane didn't describe the onset of the "dream" as she'd recalled it. Instead, she said she was on the bed but got up and walked away because the powerful sound was hurting her ears. "And then I go back and sit on the bed," she said, "I'm sitting cross-legged, and it drops in the room. The sound, it's a real thing. It's got hold of me. Vibrating."

When asked about how the globe came into the room, Jane began crying and described an entirely different scene. "They're standing in front of me," she said, describing a group of human-looking men. "They're in white clothes, and very tall. They're watching my reactions. I'm standing barefoot on a cold, shiny floor. The sound's coming in my chest, a vibrating sound they're all making. They're all looking at me intently. They're tall and pale."

When the hypnotist asked if she knew them as

friends, Jane said, "They're not enemies. They're talking, telling me their energy's going in it [the vibrating sound]. That I'm anointed. That whatever hard times may come, to have courage. That there would be times when I most need the shell to protect me. But I have to learn to help build it. And that not even the most solid shell could help protect from some of the stuff, but it would do me well to at least attempt it.... And that I will be frightened at times, but that fear is transitory and that it doesn't really hurt me.... Oh," she said suddenly, "but now I have to go in the other room! The doors open up funny and disappear. The room's so bright!"

Jane then described a brilliant "room made of light" that felt like a "cocoon." She sat and was "studied" by one of the tall, pale men. This one had light hair, although the others had hair of various jewel-like colors. They mentally discussed the things she "knows" but cannot access consciously. He told her that the knowledge would "come" to Jane when she was "ready," explaining that "each energy has to be built up, strengthened, before it can withstand the whole thing. It has to be adjusted to move in different ways of coping and seeing, and that's not easy because there are clumps of resistance in all of us."

When asked if this unexpected scenario was related to the dream of the UFO and the desert-like mesa incident with which the regression had begun, Jane said that it was, although she didn't make that connection clear. "The tan world is a representation of reality," she said, "and the different subtle shadings show how they could each fade into one another to make a whole, but yet are different. It is an actual place, yet it's a representation and symbolic. It is within our grasp. We can reach it. I went there with help."

Jane described the UFO as a device making "an observation" of her. "My ability to break out of the somnambulism and to speak shows my strength, and they were pleased," she said. "They [the tall beings] came in then to escort me out of it because I had shown that I could be strong enough."

"Were you aware of being in the tan dream in your physical body?" the hypnotist asked, and Jane said she was.

"If someone had come to your house and looked in," the hypnotist persisted, "you would not have been there in your physical form?"

"I don't know," she replied. "I was really there, it was real. My body was there."

Not much more was elicited about the UFO dream in the regression. But in Jane's first hypnosis session she remembered a series of events in rather detailed clarity. This abduction occurred when she was a young child staying with her grandmother, and her first awareness of something strange was seeing her "Nannie" collapse on the ground outside while hanging up the laundry. Suddenly, Jane felt that she was being watched and turned to see a group of four or five entities coming toward her.

When she asked why they were there, she was told, *Don't worry, you'll be all right.* And the beings escorted her toward the barn.

"What does your friend look like?" the hypnotist asked. "Is he as tall as you? Taller?"

"Just a little," she replied. "He's yellow."

Jane's memory of the following events was patchy and confused. She thought the main entity led her into the barn where she was placed in something like a "bucket" and swung around. After this, she recalled being physically examined, helped down naked from a table, and taken into a different room by the "friend" with "dark, slanted eyes."

"It's round and bright, bare," Jane described. "I see colors, just colors. The top is blue, dark royal blue. It's a pretty, blue ceiling. The floor tickles my feet, tingly. We walk through the room and come to where all the animals are."

When asked more about the animals, including a deer which she pets, she suddenly skipped to a scene of her crying beside Nannie again, still immobile slumped over the clothes basket. Once Jane was calmed down from this, the hypnotist took her back through the entire scenario. This time, Jane could see more about the examination and other details.

"When the bucket stops moving, where are you?" she was asked.

"They help me out and sit me on the table," Jane said. "It's the table. I've always been good before. *Why are you crying so much?* I don't know. He says I'll get over that. I won't feel so bad, when I get older."

"What won't feel so bad?"

"Their coming, their visits. It's so kind. They look at the right side and the left side. They lay me down, pick up my legs one at a time. It tickles. They pull my toes. And rub their hands up my sides and say, *Turn,* so I turn."

The exam continued, in which Jane was "poked" with an instrument that reminded her of "chapstick." Then she was taken into the colorful room and from there to a third location.

"We go into the room with all the green, it's so

pretty," she described. "I see big plants and animals and colors, too, of flowers and beautiful trees. I see rabbits, and I see a deer, and a bird, and...uh, oh, oh, down there in the water!"

"What water?"

"There's water, a lot of water. It's like a huge swimming pool. Something's swimming in the water, but I want to see the deer. I walk over, I see its eyes. It's white."

"What about the water?" the hypnotist asked, because Jane had turned away from that image very nervously.

"I know what's in there, and I don't want to look!" Jane resisted. "I don't want to look!

"You don't have to look," the hypnotist reassured her, but the image was already clear.

"I don't know what it is. Its head is real big, it's green," Jane said apprehensively, and then in a panic she shouted, "Oh! Oh! Ow, it's got me! Ooohhh! It has me by the neck! Ow! Let me go! Oh, oh! My ear! My ear hurts now!"

Jane was so upset by the recollection that after she had regained a calmer state of mind the session was brought to a close. Afterward, she described the water creature as having a long neck and some sort of "knobs" on its head. Something painful happened to her ear, and then the creature disappeared back into the water. She remembered nothing more, until the entities took her back to her grandmother, who then recovered consciousness. To date, whenever she has tried to read the transcripts of both regressions, she becomes so physically and emotionally upset that she cannot do it. But these are fairly mundane events within the abduction scenario, and her overreaction may come from events which are still suppressed in her memory.

Far more pleasant, or at least acceptable, have been the telepathic communications and "knowings" that have come to Jane without the aliens being present. The very first message came on November 25, 1992, from which she recorded, "I have suddenly understood that I must give myself to the Awakening. I understood this as if it were being told to me. There is a strong sense of urgency. I must respect my mother and all other things. To not hurt things, to live and let live. The time will come when they will present themselves to me in my reality. Won't be long. As angels they are in the mists of our mind. Give myself to the awakening. Do things in a good and calm matter, and everything will be okay."

The second message, on December 1, gave instructions and warned her to prepare to photograph the UFOs, which showed up as promised.

On April 22, 1993, she had another revelation. "I 'understand' I'm to get all my notes together for Karla and her work," she wrote. "What I have will be very helpful to her and is to be given freely as she asks. I'm to make special efforts to share all with her. She is very important as a voice that will introduce increased realization throughout the world. She is one of many who introduce the awareness to awakening."

The next message, on June 8, concerned something for which Jane felt she was being prepared or taught. "I understand if I meditate on my prayer list for healing at least once a day, then I will be shown results," she recorded. "That is the next step in my progression of activation. How far it will go will be determined by my level of discipline, passion, desire, and will."

On June 27, Jane woke from a dream about UFOs, but she couldn't recall any details. She did recall, however, coming to partial consciousness in the midst of the dream and trying to retain its details for later when she would be awake. But all she could remember was the briefest scene. "At one point I was standing looking at myself, and another time myself was behind me," she wrote that morning. But the notes were interrupted just then as a sudden realization came into her mind. It wasn't exactly the same as when the previous "communications" occurred, but it felt akin to that.

"All of a sudden I can remember the dream lesson given to me last night," Jane said. "It was illustrated and demonstrated to me the truth that I am truly a spiritual being animating a body. I am something separate from the body. The body is a tool, and I am entrapped in it. But I can separate from the body before death, and have done it many times, without conscious knowledge. I am a pure spiritual being when without the body, and I will be again. Patience is required. I am a spiritual being only animating a shell. The body is nothing, the soul is all."

On September 30, a telepathic communication told Jane that she was now "ready for the next level" and "the beginning of other things." She was told that some suppressed memories and information would be allowed to emerge "so I may retrieve that which will carry me forward." She saw herself as "a single mirror of mankind, aware of choosing either to "uplift" or "tear down" by her actions and intentions.

The following month, Jane experienced two more communications. "I understand I'm to attempt to rid myself of all violent and negative tendencies, to let go of controlling impulses," she was told during the first one. And the second one was simply, "I understand truth is a lonely territory. Truth is lonely. Each to his own. To disdain is incorrect."

Jane had a recent flashback that seemed to fulfill the promise made in one of the communications, about the release of suppressed memories. It concerned the UFO "dream" of December 31, 1992, and the saucer that transformed into a globe, came up close to her face, and forced her to fall. The new memories filled in the details much differently, however. After first watching a black saucer-shaped craft drop "from the clouds like a cookie cutter," Jane sensed "several intelligences" in the ship. Next, she saw it descend and transform into the sphere with four legs and designs inscribed on its surface, from which she now sensed a single intelligence. In its third permutation, the object "rose up and turned into a gray-black sphere with antennae" but no legs.

"I remember the dark, gun-metal-gray globe with antennae," she described, "having an intelligent awareness of me. When its attention came full on me, it took me over and there was nothing but me and it. Its physical force was like a huge wind without noise pushing against me. When I said hello, it was pleased and responded to me. When its attention came on me, I was its sole interest. It...was focusing entirely and completely on me.

"The antennae 'disappeared' when it came up close. There was an eye, large, and a round, silver metal thing in the area of a 'nose.' I hear metal clinks and the silver thing comes up to my ear. It feels 'clinical.' He's telling me everything is okay and he

146

knows I'm not afraid, but I'm reassured telepathically. I know they hear me, and also he's 'reading' me. There is the absolute feeling of immense power and a rather impersonal caring and kindness. I also feel concern, but again, personal yet impersonal to a great degree. As I dwell on it, the 'eye' was truly alien, or rather not human. God, it was intense, probing, objective, impersonal, all-powerful.

"The silver metal thing is looking. It connects to my ear by clamping on the outside. In fact, it clamps on and covers my entire ear, and something is inserted. Something that implants and affects my brain chemicals and certain subtle functions. It is adding. The implant looks like a very tiny oblong cylinder about a quarter-inch long or smaller, made of non-metal stuff.

"I'm reassured during the entire procedure. And it doesn't hurt too much. I ask why they need that, and he looks deep into my eyes for a long time. Then he says that it was my choice, that I agreed to all this a long time ago.

"I said I didn't remember the agreement and when did I do that. And he answered, *Before you were born*, and *we've had this conversation before*.

"I asked him, 'Why me?'

"He said, *Because you became open and now the awakening has begun*. He told me that neither I nor the many others awakened could stop the arousal of ourselves or of humankind. The trigger had been pulled, and everything was to schedule.

"They pulled the thing away from my ear, and it hurt and stung for a little bit. I felt like something had been drawn out, an energy of some sort. They inserted sound in my head, and for a little bit afterward I was blind and could only see brilliant, revolving, iridescent colors so intense I had a momentary light explosion accompanied by a brief, unbelievable wave of head pain. But I saw his eye come close, his head touching my head, our left eyes almost touching, and the pain stopped. His eye was all I could see. His eye took the colors and pain away, and I was so grateful. His eye made me sleepy. I was comforted by the closeness of the energy and by his eye.

"I can't say yet what he looked like because the 'globe' screen is strong. The globe had seams of some sort. The eye is partially outlined in some fashion...a black void, liquid somehow and observing me on all levels of my being.

"At one point during all this, but I can't remember when, I was also told that the power-hungry governments of the earth were going to be very surprised because their worst nightmare was about to come true, that even they hadn't fully estimated the effect the Voyagers' arrival would have on the worldwide human population, or the rapid growth of their influence; that they (govt.) still hadn't fully accepted that it was a losing battle and eventually they will acquiesce."

The implications of such statements, if true, are enormous. Jane didn't know what to think about the communication, although the exam scenario seemed real. Moreover, the memory differed from the spiritual encounter that emerged in the hypnotic recall. Were they two episodes of the same event, or was one memory a contrived screen for the other?

Throughout everything she has experienced, Jane's thoughts and emotions have run the gamut.

148

"At first I was terrified," she wrote in our initial contact, "but now I'm not. I feel whatever has happened has been not to hurt me. I feel like a piece of myself that was missing has been reconnected. I've had deep spiritual experiences and feelings since October 1992, all of a personal nature. I am uneasy sometimes, but I don't think I'm afraid any more."

In fact, she reported a very sudden change in her emotions that occurred in the winter of that year. "I went to bed afraid," she said, "and woke up the next day very detached," as if she'd been tranquilized and reassured. Her initial thoughts about the alien agenda, however, still made a "knot" in her stomach. "It's really all for their purpose," she said, "something that was prepared and developed long ago." And she felt she had been somehow given a choice to accept them, although it doesn't matter to them. "Either way, they win."

Jane didn't know why she was taken for alien involvement, nor what exactly she had been trained or prepared to do. Her only clue is a sense that she is "supposed" to introduce people close to her to the reality of alien existence. "You know, sometimes I feel used," she commented. "Is all this of my free will for good, or am I a puppet?"

She did feel that the aliens have put information into a deeper level of her mind, as if she were "stuffed full" with suppressed knowledge. Further, she said she didn't feel ready to know until now. She saw herself as "one of millions in a grassroots movement who are being stimulated" into a "gradual realization." Jane also sensed that the aliens had fostered within her mind a mistrustful attitude toward the government. But she was not at all sure of

149

the source of any of the events and communications because she felt that both positive and negative entities or groups may have interacted with her.

As for the aliens themselves, she has only their actions and words to guide her assessment. Once when she telepathically asked them for a better term to call them than "alien," she was given the epithet "Voyagers," and they said that the awakening humans were being made into "harbingers of discord, discontent, revolution." Judging by their actions, Jane is not always reassured.

"We're not seeing the true intelligence behind all these scenes,' she said. The fact that they put us through episodes of "set-up scenes" and "absurd stuff" frightens her.

"I'm afraid we might find that intelligence so cold and impersonal," she said, "that it would be unbearable."

VIII

ANGIE

The youngest of the eight women in this project, Angie is a delightful, extremely intelligent woman whose conscious memories of abductions and encounters could fill a book on their own. She first contacted me after reading INTO THE FRINGE and briefly described a number of incidents in her experiences that closely paralleled many things my family and I had witnessed. As in the case of Beth, Pat, and Lisa, Angie remembered abductions involving apparently military personnel before our contact, and since that time there have been several others of a most disturbing nature.

When we first began to correspond, however, Angie was not at all concerned about the possibility of detrimental military activity. After all, the aliens who had been abducting her assured her that the humans in their company were "controlled" by them, and since Angie did not fear the aliens she likewise wasn't worried about the humans with them.

Since that time, her attitude has radically changed, for very good reason. But before examining the military encounters, it is best to begin with some background about Angie and the alien contacts.

Born in 1966, Angie has German and Scotch ancestry from her mother, and, since her father was

151

adopted, she knows nothing about that side of her family. She is married and operates a small cattle ranch with her husband, Paul, outside of a large city in Tennessee. Angie is artistically talented, working in abstracts, lithography, cartooning, and clay.

Before her first alien abduction in 1988, she knew very little about such things and had never thought they could be part of her life. She did recall a few odd incidents from her childhood when I questioned her, including a strange event when she was four. She and her father were riding in his van when a blinding flash of light filled the vehicle. Immediately after the flash, Angie remembered feeling as if she were in a long, gray tunnel, but nothing more. Since that time, except for seeing a huge fireball in the sky, she could not recall anything unusual in her life.

Until the night of July 24, 1988, that is. Angie had gone to bed as usual, and then she suddenly awoke to find herself outside in the dark, paralyzed, facing a group of beings unlike anything she'd ever seen. "They were frail, hairless white beings who had the most mesmerizing eyes," she told me, and then she was amazed to watch their "catlike" eyes "wiggle" and change shape. They stared at her, and she felt as if they were reading her mind.

"This must be a dream," she said over and over.

"You are not having a dream," one of the beings told her telepathically. "We will show you. You have to go away with us for a little while."

He pointed with one of his three fingers toward the woods, and the other beings carried Angie in that direction. Terrified as she saw her house and husband receding, she begged the creatures not to take her any further, but her pleas were ignored. Angie's panic, combined with her phobia of the dark, made her very agitated, until the leader of the group injected something in her left forearm. She began to pass out, and the last words she heard were, *Just relax a little*. The next morning, Angie found two red dots in that place on her forearm.

"That's when I accepted the possibility that I'd encountered something physically genuine," she said. "I did not understand its meaning, and I spent the rest of the day wondering about the uncanny event, about how I reacted with fear because the woods seemed so dark and scary, and mostly about those dinky three-foot-tall beings. Who were they? Angels? Elves? Fairies? Ghosts? Aliens? When I went to bed that night, their image was still fresh on my mind, but I did not have any thoughts about them ever returning for me."

But the beings did return, and they have continued to come back periodically ever since. For the next two nights, Angie had clouded memories of being with the creatures, which could have been dismissed as dreams except for the fact that she discovered more red dots on her body after both nights.

Then in August she had a conscious encounter, waking in bed to see two Grays in her room. Instantly paralyzed and calmed by their "hypnotic eyes," she floated through the house with them and outside, to an unbelievable sight. "It was a big, silvery disk with revolving red, green, and yellow lights," Angie said, "suspended about two feet above the ground and it was noiseless. When I first saw it, there was no doubt in my mind that it was a UFO. That's when I accepted the possibility that the beings were aliens."

This time, Angie was not afraid. In fact, her curiosity was aroused, so she stepped forward to touch the craft. But one of the Grays leaped in front of her and warned her not to get close while the craft was in the "discharge phase" because it could harm her.

An opening appeared in the craft, and Angie saw a handsome young man, with blond hair and a tan jumpsuit, standing inside. Teleported aboard the craft, as if "sucked into a long tunnel of electric orange light," she felt separated from her body at that time, because she could see it "tumbling and twirling along beside me and all the bones, veins, and internal organs were visible."

Inside the craft, Angie was placed in a black chair where the blond man "scanned" her visually, inducing a sensation of orgasm. She asked if he, too, were an alien, and the man smiled and nodded.

The craft began to move, forcing her body back in the chair to her consternation, as she has a great fear of flying. "Where are we?" she asked, and then a small oval window appeared on the wall. She looked out and saw "thousands of brilliant stars in the midst of deep black space, but no Earth and Moon."

Four Grays entered the room, where one of them handed a case to the blond man. He removed a glowing green ball while two of the Grays floated Angie to an odd table. The man put the ball on her abdomen and moved it in a circular pattern, growing warm. Angie felt a "tugging sensation" in that area and asked what was being done to her.

The man said she was "ripe enough" and would be able to conceive. Angie told him that she and her husband had been trying unsuccessfully to have children, and the man told her she had not done so because her "blood, immune, and genetic systems" operated differently than other humans.

"Am I part alien?" she asked, confused.

One of the Grays told her that she had been "altered a little" to fulfill a special purpose. The blond man said they had produced a "novel breed" from ova they'd taken from her. He told her she was a "Chosen One" and that her children and others so chosen would *conquer the world through mastering the power of insinuation*–a message she would be given in other encounters. Angie then became very sleepy and passed out until 9 a.m. the following morning, back in bed.

After these incredible incidents, Angie seemed to undergo an interior change. "My husband and other people started noticing I seemed calmer and less talkative and daydreamed a lot," she told me. "My husband wondered what it was that I had been inscribing into the new diary I purchased. I told him that I was only recording dreams. I desperately wanted to share my story with someone, but did not because there was no one in my personal social circle who wasn't skeptical of such issues. I feared that if I told any of them, they would question my sanity. So I kept my secret for a long time to come."

During the next few months, she had only vague memories or dreams of other encounters, and after one of these she found four red dots on her abdomen in a diamond pattern. But UFOs were not the only craft to land on her property, for on November 23 she heard the sound of helicopters and looked out to see two black choppers with Air Force insignia overhead. When one of them landed on her property, Angie grabbed a coat and raced outside. But they zoomed away before she could reach them. This was the first time helicopters had been in the area, but it wouldn't be the last.

In February 1989, she had another abduction in which she was called a "Chosen One" and was also shown a scene familiar from other abductee reports. One of the aliens touched her forehead, she said, and "a series of graphic images exploded" in her mind. She saw "a reddish-gold desert planet with two setting suns," a "galaxy," a "blood-red moon and a fiery orange sun exploding," and an "underground city" before she blacked out. When she regained consciousness, an alien told her their home was "Cassiopeia in the heavens" but that they had made a home for themselves on Earth before humans were created. After this, Angie passed out again and was returned home.

Two days later, another helicopter circled the property, and a man who claimed to work for the utility company arrived, asking to examine the two transformers on the farm. He said there had been many power failures in the area, but Angie was suspicious since she hadn't recalled any such failures nor had she contacted the utility company.

Eight nights after the last abduction, Angie recalled waking up in the back yard with four aliens. Naked–although feeling neither cold nor embarrassed–she watched two aliens working with a "car-sized" device while a third one appeared to be digging soil samples. The fourth alien showed her a small black box, which he gave her and asked her to look inside. She did, and again her mind "exploded" and was filled with images, this time abstract patterns of bright colors. He then told her that she would soon "have the power to make mental contact" with other Chosen Ones and would be able to "influence their minds," and then he touched her chest and she blacked out.

The next day when Angie went outside, she found a large circle in the grass which looked "parched" and several chunks of bubbly black metal slag. Excited by this proof, Angie photographed the metal and the circle, which didn't disappear for over a year and a half. Analysis of the metal in 1993 showed it to be ordinary iron slag.

In March she had two "cloudy" memories of abductions, both involving abdominal procedures, and in one of them she saw a group of "dazed" humans in the same room. On March 23, Angie counted nineteen helicopters flying over the farm and thought she could make out Air Force designations on them.

Ten days later, Angie recalled another abduction, but this one differed dramatically from the previous encounters. She found herself outside in the dark with a thin blue alien who "mind scanned" her. Then five men came out of the shadows, four of whom were "ordinary men wearing olive-green uniforms" with "crewcuts" and the fifth was "a dark-haired humanoid" in a long khaki coat with many pockets. This man, Angie said, "touched the blue alien and it suddenly shrank into a marble-sized orb of white light" which the humanoid then pocketed. He told her that these beings, "a nonphysical form of energy," were created and controlled by his group.

"Did you create humans, too?" Angie asked, and he confirmed this.

"What do you want from me?" she continued.

"We want to talk to you about your life," he told her.

"That's all?" she asked.

"There's more," he said, and one of the uniformed men took Angie to a black van parked behind her garage.

"Is that a real van, or is that your spaceship?" she wondered.

"You can't judge a book by its cover," another man replied cryptically.

Inside the van, Angie saw bench seats, carpet, and a large control panel. The other men entered, and Angie wondered if they belonged to some military group.

"Are you all with the Army, Air Force, Navy, or Marines," she inquired.

The oldest man replied, but she was beginning to have a hard time understanding everything he said. She thought he said the group belonged to an organization called "High Shelf" which worked mainly in "special underground stations." He also told her that she and other "Chosen Ones" were part of a mind-control project, to "carry instructions and temperance, via thought transference" to other people.

Once he answered her questions, he began an interrogation about her life. Angie could recall only a few of the questions, however, in her altered condition. He asked, for instance, if she remembered the aliens coming to her when she was young, which she did not. And he asked about her views on life and death. After the interview, which seemed quite lengthy, the man activated something on the control

158

panel, and Angie found herself back in bed, fully alert and "tingling all over," at 5:10 a.m. She quickly dressed and ran outside to see if they were still there, but the yard was empty.

Thinking about all her encounters, Angie came to several conclusions. First, she now believed that there was something much bigger than "man's views and theories and religions" to the universe. And she believed that the aliens were carrying out a "psychic transformation" with her and others for a good purpose.

Through the following months, Angie had several more encounters and UFO sightings. The most traumatic series of events began with an abduction in which she was "impregnated." Two weeks later, she took two home-pregnancy tests which proved positive, and she and her husband were elated. Angie did not tell Paul about the alien impregnation, since he had not believed her previous accounts of sightings and intrusions. She thought the baby inside her was a special gift from her alien friends, and, being unfamiliar with the typical alien process of impregnation and subsequent retrieval of the fetus, she looked forward to carrying the child to term and beginning the family which she and Paul desired. They had even selected names for the baby.

But a month after the impregnation encounter, Angie started having unusual physical symptoms: "sweating" and "tingling" during the day, and a pulsating sensation in the womb area at night. This continued for over two weeks, until on the morning of July 4, Angie suffered a bloody, painful miscarriage.

"It happened in my bathroom," she said. "After

159

hours of heavy bleeding and terrible cramping, the fetus came out, in my hands." It wasn't like a normal fetus; larger, three inches long, devoid of sex organs, and had "black, slanted" eyes reminiscent of the white aliens she had encountered. Under a strange compulsion, Angie put the fetus in a jar of water and hid it in the barn loft. Later she went back and found that the jar was missing.

Paul took Angie to the doctor right away, as she'd lost a lot of blood and subsequently she had a "D&C" procedure. She couldn't understand why she'd lost the baby, having taken excellent care of herself, and the loss was devastating.

At a much later date, Angie underwent two hypnotic regressions, in which three of her experiences were examined. One of these was the loss of the fetus, and in that regression Angie described a hitherto unremembered bedroom visitation in the hours before her miscarriage. Several beings and a large, floating blue light entered the bedroom. While some of the aliens busied themselves with Paul, two others carried out an abdominal procedure on Angie, involving a small cylindrical device that "clicked."

Nothing further intruded until September, when Angie awoke with a vague recollection of being on a craft with her sister, Julia. That morning, Julia phoned and told her, "I had the weirdest dream last night." She described being with human-looking aliens in blue jumpsuits in a curved, domed room, and she saw Angie there, too, in a silver jumpsuit like the aliens wore. She recalled Angie telling her, "They want to give us eternal life."

The same details had been part of Angie's memories, and the two sisters got together to discuss the shared "dreams." Angie told her sister then, for the first time, about her other encounters, relieved to end the "emotional isolation and fear of ridicule" that had kept her quiet before this.

Her circle of confidants expanded in November, when her father told of seeing a domed, orange UFO while out in the Smoky Mountains with some friends. Angie and Julia shared their experiences with him, and that prompted their father to open up even more. "The three of us learned a lot that day," Angie said. "I told Dad about all of my alien encounters; Dad told us about his past encounters and about our mother's experiences, too; I cried. That was the day we learned that our parents have been involved with the aliens since before we were born."

Intermittent abductions continued to occur. From December 1989 to April 1992, Angie recalled fifteen events. In one, she was shown a nursery of "clones" similar to other abductee reports, and she was told that the aliens had "programmed" her to hide the fetus after her miscarriage. When Angie asked if the aliens had restored the fetus to life, she found it hard to understand the reply that its physical body had been stored and its soul recycled.

In another, Angie was shown a "clone" infant as well as nine "hybrid tots" and was told they would be used "to prepare [humans] for the changes." When she asked, "What changes?" she was told it involved "humans' spiritual transformation."

One abduction during this time was very singular, as Angie recalled going to an underground facility that her uniformed human escort said was in northern Arizona. He told her there were other stations around the world, including bases in New

Mexico, the North Pole, and Africa. When Angie asked who was in charge of the "High Shelf" operation, another of the men, a "blond humanoid" replied that his kind "control everything."

"What about the Grays and the other aliens?" she asked, thinking of the several different types she had encountered. "Are they involved, too?"

"By degrees," he answered.

"What about all these humans?" she persisted, "these military people?"

"We control them," the blond smiled.

She was taken to a group of other abductees or "Chosen Ones" and was handed a small black box and told to open it. When she pulled open the lid, Angie said, "a mist of brilliant violet light" came out, covering the group of abductees and causing "a powerful electric sensation" after which she blacked out.

Throughout these encounters, Angie had felt positive about her involvement with the aliens, including, finally, the loss of her unborn child, which she believed was for a higher purpose. And in the abduction she and Julia remembered sharing, Julia had accepted Angie's statement about getting "immortal life" from the beings, so she, too, had a positive attitude. It was surprising, therefore, that Julia was extremely frightened a month later when the sisters spotted a UFO.

Returning from Georgia on December 29, they were driving along a state highway in Tennessee. At 7:30 p.m. they saw two unusual vehicles. The first one, Angie described as "an old spray-painted bus" traveling very slowly, "full of hippie folk," with the words "Magic Bus" painted across the rear.

162

The sisters laughed about it, but then the bus slowed to about ten miles per hour, and Angie could not pass it as they moved up a hill. She and Julia saw some of the bus's occupants open their windows and shout, and then one of them pointed upward. The girls looked in that direction and saw a bright blue object above the treetops ahead. It had a dome, wide rim, and black, round portholes.

"Angie, look!" Julia shouted. "That's a UFO!"

The hippie bus accelerated and was soon out of sight, as Angie's Corvette came to a complete stop on its own. A blue glow engulfed the car.

"Oh, God! It's behind us!" Julia screamed in fear.

In Julia's account of the incident to me, she wrote, "When it came towards us, I got scared. And Angie told me there was nothing to be afraid of, but I still felt afraid and got down in the floorboard of the car."

There was a brief "intermittent beeping sound," Angie said, and "then all was silence and darkness. The UFO was gone." The car's headlights popped on, Angie turned the ignition, which worked perfectly, and started to drive away, telling Julia it was safe for her to get out of the floorboard.

"Goddammit, Angie," Julia replied, "let's go!"

They took off, and a few minutes later Julia said, "Do you know what time it is? Ten-twenty." Angie didn't believe her, but when she checked her own watch, it had the same time. Almost three hours had passed since they spotted the blue UFO, and the sisters didn't have a single memory of what transpired.

In April 1992, Paul and Angie moved onto the cattle ranch, and an entirely new series of mysterious events began. Their specialty-beef business was doing very well until something started killing off the cattle, and within a year the losses amounted to thousands of dollars.

"A small number of them had been mutilated," Angie reported. "One cow was missing a head, another had been disemboweled, and a bull calf appeared as if he'd been ripped apart by a tyrannosaur. The bodies of some of the mutilated ones had peculiar stigmata such as shaved places, clean and bloodless holes and gashes. There wasn't a single scratch anywhere on the rest of the dead cattle."

Many of the cattle died in February and March 1993, when other farmers in the general area also reported dead and mutilated animals. Reading about one of these reports, Angie contacted the paper and got in touch with a veterinarian who'd examined someone else's dead cattle. In the first case, he reported that the cattle had died of toxins of an unknown source, and with Angie's cattle, all he could report was death from unknown causes.

The alien activity after this was rather different than what had transpired before, and for the most part Angie was left with very cloudy and incomplete memories of the events. One abduction, however, is worth noting at some length.

Waking on board a craft, naked on a table, Angie saw humanoids and two different kinds of Grays. Momentarily, two more humanoids, in red suits, entered, and Angie recognized the blond one as the man she'd seen before. She asked if he had a name, and he told her "Carl De Zan."

He told her that it was time for her group of Chosen Ones to carry out their "assigned tasks." This involved making contact with "certain people throughout the world" to "collect data" from their minds. And that data, in turn, would then be collected from the minds of the Chosen Ones by the aliens. All of this would be done, he said, through tiny implants in the head, devices that served many purposes. They could help the implanted people use their "special senses," for instance, and stay in contact with one another through dreams. Besides collecting data, the implants could also send instructions.

When Angie asked about the overall purpose–the agenda–she was told that through "tempering" human minds, the aliens wanted to remove "filth and evil" and "negativity" from humans.

Having been given repeated lectures about her special abilities as a "Chosen One," at one point Angie initiated an experiment with herself. "I decided to test my mental powers by giving thought transference a try," she reported. "I went to bed around 11 p.m. and concentrated long and hard to project my image into my sister's dream. During the process, I drifted off to sleep and soon found myself in a dream in which Julia was present!

"I phoned my sister [the next morning] to let her know about my attempt at reaching her in her dream, but before I had a chance to say anything, she recounted the dream in full detail."

Angie also decided to try hypnotic regression in order to uncover anything she could about the events she'd been unable to remember consciously. Undergoing two hypnosis sessions, Angie was surprised to retrieve details of a childhood encounter in one session. Going back to age four, when she and her father had been blinded by a flash of light while riding in a van, Angie recalled being taken into a gray, cigar-shaped craft where she saw several men and women in white coats. One man with "long, dark blond hair" took charge of her, carrying the crying child to a strange table.

"It's metal and has an edge around it," she described, "like for blood to drain off. And there is something down at the foot, under the table, but I can't see it clearly."

Acting in what she perceived as a "hurried" manner, the man strapped her wrists down as she lay on the table and placed on her head a "headband thing" with moving red and yellow lights. The hypnotist instructed Angie to view the scene from a distance, rather than reliving it, and she obliged.

"I can see my hands twitching," she said. "The wristbands are making my fingers twitch and jerk. I'm lying there with the headband on, and my eyes are open. The pupils are dilated like I'm dead."

She then described a procedure in which a clear tube was inserted vaginally and filled with "a pinkish liquid" as one of the women pressed on Angie's abdomen. When she was revived, the blond man tried to "jolly" her out of her terrified state, and she was returned to the van, which exited the cigar-shaped craft by flying out of the opening "on its own," as Angie reported.

"We're coming down to the road," she said, "I can see it clearly because it's daytime, and the van lands smoothly on the road. It's moving by itself for a minute, and that's when I notice it's going in the wrong direction. We were going the other way before they took us."

"What is your father doing now?" the hypnotist

asked.

"He sort of shakes his head," she said, "like he's perplexed, and he keeps driving."

In August and September 1993, Angie recalled three other encounters, including one in which she saw her father aboard the same craft. When she questioned him, he described an abduction memory from that same night, although he didn't recall seeing Angie. In another, she was given information about alien life in other parts of the galaxy, about their travel technology, and about their having created life forms on Earth, including humans.

But the next month, the abduction and encounter scenarios changed abruptly, beginning on October 2, when Angie woke up and found herself downstairs in a guest room with "a youthful male humanoid" wearing "an oversized red plaid shirt, faded jeans, and black leathery boots." Angie felt in control of her senses, unlike some previous situations, and asked the young man several questions, including his origins. In spite of his very human appearance, he told her he and his kind were "extraterrestrials" and wanted to know if the term made her feel uneasy.

"No," she replied, "I'm not afraid of you any more." She could see a silvery disk outside the house and assumed she would be taken there, but instead the man embraced her and she became partially paralyzed from the chest up. Then he lay her on the floor and had intercourse with her, after which she felt faint and passed out.

She remembered this occurring again, on the nights of October 3 and 4, and on the morning after the October 3 encounter Angie awoke with blood dripping from her nostril and increasing congestion and pain in her shoulder. In spite of this, she had not been upset by the three encounters, and since the intercourse had not been frightening, she wondered why the man had induced the partial paralysis and subsequent loss of consciousness.

Four nights later, she went through an encounter that was far less pleasant. Angie went to bed very late that night, around 1:30 a.m., and folded her clothes neatly on a bedside table before turning out the light. In what seemed like only a few minutes later, she awoke fully alert, listening to the sound like a jet engine that was loud and getting louder. Her next perception was that she was not in the bedroom, but rather standing completely dressed in an unfamiliar grassy clearing in the woods near an old dirt road. And she wasn't alone. "With me were three apparently frightened young women," Angie described. "One was lying face-down in the grass weeping."

Angie became frightened herself, for the first time since her initial abduction. "My instincts said that we were about to be abducted by a force so great that we would not be able to control our situation no matter how hard we might pray to God."

One of the other women, tall and plump and brown-haired, started yelling, "Here they come! Here they come!"

The sound grew unbearable as a strange-looking airplane flew toward them and landed like a helicopter. Two of the women panicked and ran into the woods, while Angie and the brunette stood frozen in place by fear. A group of men in black uniforms emerged and began rounding up all the women. As they were hurried toward the craft, Angie said she remembered "telling them that I'm not an animal and do not appreciate them treating me like one."

Ignoring her, the men pushed the women into narrow compartments at the rear of the craft, which then took off and frightened Angie even more with its erratic flight. She began to pray and then blacked out.

"After coming to my senses," Angie reported, "I found myself sitting in a chair and at some place that looked like a military base. I saw several men in military uniforms leading some humans toward these long, gray buildings. "

Two men took Angie into one of the buildings, where she saw a group of people seated around a conference table, some in uniform and others in ordinary clothing. One of the men, who had on a uniform with many decoration ribbons, stared at Angie wordlessly from the table and engaged her in a brief telepathic conversation. Then a woman came up behind Angie, and when she turned to look at her, the woman's gaze paralyzed her. The woman gave Angie a dark red liquid to drink, which made her dizzy and sleepy to the point of passing out. After that, she remembered only a brief view of the buildings from a distance and then the sound of the strange aircraft once again.

When Angie underwent hypnosis, she chose to examine this experience, recovering a few more details. After passing out from the bitter liquid, Angie recalled waking up in one of five chairs that seemed to be on a stage or platform. "A man and three women were sitting in chairs at both sides of me," she said. "I experienced physical paralysis and couldn't think straight when the general gazed into my eyes. He wasn't any more than two inches from my face.

He lifted my hand, then dropped it, like checking to see if I was in a deep trance, then checked my pupils. He did the same with the others. The woman presented a small reddish-brown box to him," she continued, "and he pulled out a tube from underneath it and attached the tube to something between my chair and the next person's. I blacked out again and have absolutely no memories of what transpired during the remaining time I was there."

When she got out of bed the next morning, her neatly folded clothes were scattered on the floor. She had a hissing sound in one ear and problems hearing the rest of the day. And she discovered the door to the basement standing open that morning. When Angie called the next day to tell me about this incident, I could hear helicopters flying over her home. She had been very unnerved by the incident and said it was all "scary and confusing."

That fear turned to sheer terror the following month, when once again Angie was forcefully taken by men in military uniforms from her bedroom. Earlier that day, November 9, another dead cow was found in the barn. The body was unmarked, but blood had seeped from its nose and mouth. There was no sign of a struggle, however.

That night after going to sleep, Angie awoke to go to the bathroom, and immediately she heard helicopters approaching. From the bathroom window she looked out, but she saw nothing and could no longer hear the choppers. Angie went back to bed and to sleep, but woke up again hearing not only the helicopters but also the sound of a vehicle coming up the drive.

She tried to rouse Paul, but he wouldn't wake up.

170

The back door opened, and Angie went "limp" when a group of men in olive-drab jumpsuits came in to the bedroom. Paul started to stir, but one of the men touched him with a wand-like device and Paul stopped moving.

The men took Angie outside where two green helicopters were hovering. She was put inside one of them, given an injection, and told she was being taken in "for evaluation." She was also fitted with a chest and shoulder device from which a breathing tube was placed in her mouth for the duration of the flight, perhaps twenty minutes. The chopper landed in a rural area with buildings and many helicopters in view. Military personnel were busy on the grounds, some leading civilians, perhaps other abductees, through the base.

"A gray van approached our helicopter," Angie told me, "and stopped about twenty yards ahead of us. Two men in olive-drab suits exited the rear of the vehicle, and then a third one came out with a tall, slim man in a pinstripe shirt. The fellow with the striped shirt had metal cuffs on his wrists and white tape over his mouth, and appeared to be in a state of panic. Two men carrying black rifles came into the scene," she continued. "That grieving man was pushed to the ground, and one of the armed men pumped one bullet into his back."

In complete terror, Angie was then carried over to where the man's body lay. She asked why "they had to kill that poor man."

"You talked," one of the men said.

"But what's this got to do with him?" she asked.

"We take one like him each time a recruit talks," he told her.

"You could have wasted me instead," Angie replied, but the man said she was too valuable as part of an alien "project" involving implants.

She said she knew they were trying to brainwash her and make her fear them, but the man said they only wanted to keep her in line. He told her that she would be forced to watch more such killings if she continued to "talk to Karla Turner" about her experiences, and that more of her cattle would also be killed.

She was then taken into a building and underwent a series of physical procedures, including blood-taking, a shower of some sort, and a gynecological exam, before being returned home.

Angie was extremely angry and frightened by the experience, and I was concerned for her safety when she told me about it. By that time, I had begun this book project, and I asked Angie if she wanted to withdraw from it. But she refused to be intimidated by the threats and continued to cooperate with me.

Four nights later, the men in military uniforms returned, and Angie was flown to an area near a hillside where she was taken into an underground facility. She was given an injection, followed by a shower to remove some brown dust that had gotten on her earlier, and then by another gynecological procedure. She was told that she and some other women there were part of "a genetic experiment which involves cloning and DNA replication."

After this she was escorted to another area where several tables were covered by plastic sheeting, which one of the medical women removed. "I recall seeing two large control panels and two large metal crates near the table," Angie said. "The medical woman told me that they call it the 'table of screams' because a lot of women who have been put there freak out when they get a look at some of the 'probes' that are used."

Placed on the table, Angie was fitted with a headphone-type device that emitted a loud beeping, and she temporarily lost consciousness. When she came to, she was face-down on the table but able to move. "A small silver box with the open end towards me sat just a few inches from my face," she said. "Inside the box was a gray and white mechanical device of some sort which made clicking sounds. The lady came around in front of me and poked a thin, black rod into the side of the mechanical device. She said, 'It's been deprogrammed. We've never had this sort of thing happen before'."

Angie asked if they were doing something with the implant in her head and was told "that there was more than one implant device in there, that two were the aliens' products and one came from them."

Angie asked, "Why in hell have you gone and stuck implants in my body? What are they for?"

The medical woman told her that the aliens do different things with them that her group couldn't discern. "They won't give us all their knowledge, I'm sure you understand that by now," Angie reported the woman as saying.

Having encountered a number of physically different aliens, Angie asked which ones the woman meant. She was told that the military group was involved with some groups of aliens but not with two of the groups who had contacted Angie. She said the military group's implants "monitor how many times [implanted abductees] come into contact with alien beings" as well as recording "the approximate location of a pick-up."

In the course of further procedures, Angie was held down while the women inserted a probe into her left nostril. When they performed a second test, Angie was told that the alien implants had "deprogrammed" those from the military group.

Her next recollection is of being taken to a room with other women where they were all interrogated by an older man in an officer's uniform whom she remembered as a major. According to Angie, the major said, "You people are going to tell me everything. I don't want to be an asshole and force it out of you, but if that's what it takes...."

Three women were questioned before Angie, and when her turn came she was asked about the information she'd been given by the Whites and Grays about their implants. She told him that she'd seen four kinds of Grays and didn't know which ones had used the implants on her.

"You're lying," the major replied. "I'm going to ask you one more time."

"Which aliens do you want to know about?" she asked. "I told you I've been with a lot of them."

"Start with the slender gray aliens," he told her. "Did any of those talk about implants?"

"I can't think," she said, "you're confusing me." It was her way of evading his questions because she felt it was "none of his business."

He ordered that she be taken to another area called the "probing room," where she lost consciousness after receiving another injection.

After each abduction by the military group, Angie grew more and more apprehensive and fearful. When I asked her about any positive help she might have

174

received from the aliens she thought of as her friends, Angie's reply, in a January 2, 1994, letter, showed how much more she now questioned her experiences than she had done in the beginning.

"Since that military group stepped into the scene," she wrote, "there haven't been any aliens to come to my rescue. I constantly pray for help and guidance from the good sources in the universe, but there just hasn't been any help on my part. I don't know which aliens are trying to help me, and which aliens are out to deceive me. The spiritual growth and all the good things I've experienced may not be linked to my [alien] experiences. Maybe it's just something I brought about all by myself."

Apparently there was someone else aware of her feelings, because six days after she wrote that letter Angie had an alien abduction for the first time in months, which seemed designed, in part, to placate her. After going to bed on the night of January 8, she woke up to find herself on board a craft in the company of a Gray. Angie said she was neither paralyzed nor in a trance state and clearly recalls the alien using some device to "locate and reactivate an implant" by insertion of something into her ear. She was then told they were finished with her and she would be returned home.

"Before I go," Angie said, "you are going to tell me what this is all about."

The alien replied that information had just been placed in the implant and that Angie would "know everything in due time." But she insisted on asking more questions. When she asked why the military personnel had given her so many injections, the alien said that they used "tranquilizer drugs on all recruits to prevent them from running away." She said the alien also apologized for the military group's "indiscretions" and told her she would not be made to watch any more "killing events."

Angie had her doubts about this and told the alien that the warning had been for her not to "talk," but that she had continued to "talk" since then. The alien replied that she should do what she felt was important. "He said the military people have been untruthful about most of what they've told me," she reported, "and that some of their demonstrations were mere illusions. It's part of their cover-up."

She also questioned him about the space craft and was told that it operated on "the power of the mind." But she was unable to ask anything more because four Grays entered and led her through a corridor to an exit from the craft just then.

"I saw that we were in a big hangar at some base," she said, "and there must have been more than fifty military people there."

She was told that those people would return her to her home, but before she could go over to them, one of the aliens used some device to render her unconscious. Her next memory was of being back in her bedroom, and that day she had recurrent bouts of pain on the side of her head where the probe had gone into her ear.

As with most abductees, there is no ending yet to Angie's story, nor a clear understanding of the agenda behind her repeated abductions. But there are certainly a number of important questions raised by her account, which has only been partially presented here.

Compared to other abduction scenarios, Angie's

contains many of the typical elements: various physical exams, fetus-retrieval and baby presentation; visions of the desert world; sexual activities; training and instruction sessions; teleportation methods; the "black box"; punctures and bruises; and implants, to name a few. Similarly, her reports of activities and details in the encounters involving apparently military personnel contain much that is familiar from other accounts.

What is very untypical, however, is the richness of her recollections. In most abductions, the person can only remember small parts of the total event, and this is true for Angie, too, in many of the encounters. But in some of them she seems to have been allowed to retain more than the usual level of awareness. Either that, or she just naturally is not as susceptible at times to the mind-control procedures which are used to suppress abductees' memories.

The abundance of information she received is also untypical. Certainly there are many abductees who have been instructed on various topics in the same way Angie had been. But she has managed to retain an enormous amount of this information which can be correlated with the numerous but more incomplete reports from other cases, on such topics as mind-control methods, alien-human collusion, and implant capabilities.

Still, she doesn't recall everything, as she has noted and as hypnosis has shown. So why is she allowed to recall these particular things? Is this programmed or accidental? If programmed, by whom, and for what purpose?

Further questions are raised by a contradiction in the details of two related recent events. It concerns the controversial subject of covert cooperation between human agencies and alien groups. When Angie and the other women were questioned by the major, he focused at one point on what Angie knew about the implants of the Whites and Grays. This implied that his organization was not familiar with those kinds and thus not allied in any way. Angie had also been told that the military group worked with some aliens but not with all of them.

But in the January 8 abduction, Angie was aboard a craft with one of the Grays, who proceeded to discuss the military group in a negative manner. This implied that he was not allied with them. Yet, when that craft landed, Angie saw they were inside a military facility.

Some further explanation is clearly called for to resolve the confusion. From what she has observed of relations between our military organization, whatever its aegis, and their alleged alien allies, Angie thinks they are at odds in some ways. Her impression is that the human organization is responsible for the extreme cover-up activities rather than the aliens. But this is based in part upon one of the aliens' statement that they had no concern about their presence being known—a dubious statement, however, given their employment of memory suppression and virtual reality illusions.

Given the aliens' VRS capabilities, there is always a question of the reality of these events. Just recently, however, Angie's husband told her he'd had a strange dream that some men broke into the house and took her away. Unhappily, she had had the same dream that night.

Angie is keenly aware of the unanswered

questions. "Although some of my experiences with them have led to a positive transformation," she once said, "the aliens certainly are not any more open with me now than they were five years ago....

"Until I undergo hypnosis and some truth is recovered, there's no way of my really knowing right now which aliens are trying to help me and which aliens are trying to deceive me. All of them seem to handle things clandestinely, even the good ones, and they're all alien in actions and appearance as far as I can tell.

"It could very well be that some types are experimenting on me for their own benefit and are lying to me just like they are lying to other people. I just don't think this is the case with all alien types I've encountered. I would want to think that at least one group is trying to help instead of harm and deceive me.

"I've learned to wash my hands of blind faith and am now beginning to use my God-given reasoning faculties and extreme caution, reasoning, and prayer in deciding how I should respond to the aliens," Angie said. "I am a human being, and we humans do have feelings and rights!"

IX

Amy

Of all the contacts I received after INTO THE FRINGE was released, Amy's first letter was the most compelling. She wrote, as she explained, because it was the only way to get free of a compulsion that had begun in November 1992, after an extraordinary dream. The following week, she bought and read my book, and then began the compulsion to write me and share the dream.

Amy, however, as I would find out, has a strong sense of independence, self-control, logic, skepticism, and an admirable stubbornness. She resisted the "ridiculous" compulsion for several months, but by April she was ready to get it out of her system and reasoned that writing the letter would end it.

In the first part, Amy described some unusual events that corresponded with things I related in INTO THE FRINGE. These included odd phone behavior, which she humorously attributed to "The Phantom of the Opera-tor," and unexplained electrical problems and noises in the house. None of the unusual experiences were attributed to alien activity, a glaring absence in comparison to the other contacts I'd gotten. But then she began to describe the dream. In the first scene, Amy and her daughters were in a campground where "huge tarantulas" chased them. They got in the car and drove away, but the car started flying upward, over the trees, where she saw a huge moon.

"In front of the moon," she wrote, "I saw the silhouettes of some small, thin beings. They had big heads like the aliens I've heard about, and they were moving about in front of the moon or light that glowed behind them. One turned and looked at me, and I saw large, black eyes. I wasn't afraid of him. I thought, *Well, I've never actually seen one of them—now I know what they look like.*"

She heard a loud noise approaching, and then she flew onto a metal-roofed house. "I knew the metal might be hot," she noted, "so I knew not to touch it." Amy was on the second story, where she looked through "large windows" into one of the rooms. There she saw a group of men talking excitedly and heard a softer, female, voice telling them to "calm down because there was work to do." The men looked human, but the female was part of "a group of non-Earth representatives."

When she was brought into the room, she said, "The humans introduced me to a female alien wearing a white plastic mask so that her appearance would not frighten the others and so they wouldn't focus on her eyes. Even though she wore a mask, I could see her eyes through the holes in the mask. They were big, black eyes. From that point on, I remember being right next to her, and her face stayed very close to my face...very intense!"

The first part in the campground was either a natural dream or a screened sequence, but the illusory force rapidly disappeared as she moved from the campground to the room in the alien's company.

181

Amy said the alien explained that her race had been doing things to humans that they should not be doing. "She and several groups of her race wanted to stop the 'abuse' of the humans by her race. They were working with certain people on Earth to stop the process. The other humans in the room were ex-pilots, military officials, and other professionals."

I was riveted, now, because Amy's account echoed that of information I'd recently received, from two widely separated sources, about a covert program or effort by certain parties in the intelligence and military organizations to resist alien abductions and to assist abductees in certain ways.

There was no doubt in my mind that some in the military had an active hand in monitoring and questioning abductees, as my husband Casey had gone through such an experience. Other abductees—including Leah Haley and Debbie Jordan—had also reported contacts, intrusions, and kidnappings by human, seemingly military, agents, and there was objective evidence in some cases to back up the reports. But this was a far cry from accounts of human agents actively helping abductees, much less a coalition of human and alien parties working against the abduction agenda, as the information alleged to come from the intelligence community has claimed. So far as I knew, this claim was not generally known from public ufological material. Yet here it was in Amy's dream.

Her account went on to say that the masked alien dominated Amy's attention, "putting" information directly into her mind. "She explained all kinds of things, but I don't remember it all," Amy wrote. "I think I remember my role in the plan, but I don't like knowing so I forget. I don't want to remember!

"After she told me about those things, she told me about implants. She put a thin, pencil-like metal instrument in my right ear and I thought, *Oh! This is gonna hurt!* but I couldn't move or stop her. To my surprise, it didn't hurt! She pulled out the instrument, and on one end was a flat, circular, small, flesh-colored...thing. It was...reddish colored but sort of transparent. If I looked closely I could see something inside the thing.

"This part," Amy stressed, "when she pulled that thing out of my ear, was the most real seeming, the most clear and most intense part of my dream. It was very important that I remember! I think she said that to me."

Amy said the alien explained certain things about the implant, and then she bent over while the alien removed a second implant from Amy's neck. It was a "dark, cylindrical" object about "three centimeters long" with "something sticking on the end of it like very fine wires." The alien then explained how the implant operated.

"She showed me the thing she had pulled out of my neck," Amy reported, "and said, *This is embedded deep into the spinal cord.* I can't remember exactly what she explained about it, but I think the thing controlled the muscles of the body when activated. It blocked the brain and became the 'central command' of the body. She also said that sometimes these things were implanted into a person's lower back somewhere between the fourth lumbar and the sacrococcygeal, but it was more commonly 'planted' in the neck. I don't want to remember how or why this thing functioned."

The alien told Amy more about the implants, about her group's efforts to remove them from abductees, and other things Amy couldn't recall.

"I remember that she was sorry for what some of 'her people' had done," Amy wrote, "but she–and others–were trying to help. The last thing I remember was that she was showing me something on a very large TV or computer screen or window."

Amy then concluded her letter, saying that when she read my book she thought she should share the dream with me, although it felt "ridiculous" to write to someone about a "dream." She made no claims for the dream, nor for having any actual alien experiences, and she did not ask for any advice, help, or response. Clearly, Amy had written the letter only to make the compulsion "stop bugging" her.

I didn't need an invitation to respond, however, as her information was too compelling to ignore. Amy had commented that "certain elements of my dream resembled parts of your book," but when I read back through the dream I could see very little actual similarity other than the facts that my husband had seen military people in an abduction and that I had recalled an ear implant. I suspected there were other details she hadn't shared, however, because people very often hold back from the entire truth when first "testing the waters" with someone they don't know. And not only was I intrigued by the content of the dream, I was also curious to know more about Amy's potential situation because she lived in the very same city where my family and I lived during the experiences I wrote about in FRINGE. Finally there was the fact of her compulsion to contact me rather than some other researcher, and the possibility that our contact was being directed.

I got her number from information and phoned as soon as possible. I learned that she was a divorced mother of two young daughters who had just finished her master's degree in counseling. She was born in Dallas in 1953, of Scotch, Irish, English, and French ("Cajun") ancestry and had lived most of her life in the Metroplex area. Amy was truly surprised by my interest. In fact, as she later confessed humorously, she wondered if I were "one taco short of a full combo plate" for being "interested in a dream."

Amy did agree, however, to share more information about many of her experiences, which she confessed were rather "fringe-like" even though they didn't in conscious reality involve aliens or UFOs. I asked her to describe any past unusual events, of any sort, and a few weeks later she complied, with a list of psychic, dream, telepathic, and miscellaneous experiences.

"It was a lot harder [to make the list] than I expected," she said. "It was like trying to see through a dense fog. I've always kept these things at a distance from my awareness."

That distance was rapidly diminishing, and in the course of the next several months, we explored together her memories and the accounts found in the journals she had kept for many years. Amy's progressive self-rediscovery is a story of its own. Layer after layer of repression and denial were stripped away as she read back through the journals and realized that some powerful phenomenon had been part of her life from the beginning.

Even as young as four, Amy had a feeling of "influence" from an unseen source. By seven, she had recognized this source more directly, calling it the "Many in One" because she could hear many people speaking in unison. In adolescence Amy called this force the "Council."

"At first I only heard them talking to one another, not to me," she explained. "I have only heard them audibly a few times, like when they told me my mother was going to die (she did) and other events that would happen in the future (the events did happen)," she explained. "I usually sense a dialogue of symbols, images, and concepts. When I 'listen,' I forget how to speak, words cease to exist, and I forget what using vocal cords feels like. I call it the 'language without words.' No trance states."

She also had a brief yet vivid memory of seeing a small, dark figure move rapidly into her bedroom doorway and crouch down one night. And when she was ten, Amy recalled walking alone into a field near her house very early one morning. She had no idea why she was going there, and she couldn't remember what happened when she arrived nor much about her return home.

In 1965, Amy dreamed of being in the back yard and waving goodbye to a UFO hovering above her, and the next moment she woke up surprised to be in her bed. The dream felt so real that she got up to see if the UFO was still nearby. It should be recalled, incidentally, that 1965 was a major "flap" year for UFO sightings and encounters throughout the country.

A few months later, Amy went through a sudden internal change of attitudes and interests, began to study the sciences, and blossomed intellectually in school. The psychic element also grew increasingly stronger, and in her later teenage years Amy started having many dreams of an unknown "lady" teaching her intensely about a number of things, beginning with levitation. Although she called them dreams, the teaching sessions had a real effect on Amy, and she once accidentally levitated a bottle of shampoo and almost frightened herself to death. When the sessions began to include instructions on affecting electrical systems, Amy sometimes witnessed the physical, external effects of her ability on appliances in her environment.

This is also the time when she accepted the fact that her existence was somehow being guided by the Council. She was led to study certain subjects and was implanted with many concepts and ideas about time, space, physics and other complex thoughts. Altogether, in fact, Amy became aware of a sense of destiny and purpose she couldn't understand but could only feel as a certainty.

"I'm scared," she noted in her journal for January 1971, "because something so unknown and powerful is pulling at me, every moment I'm caught off guard and pulled. I'm being pulled to a state or level of mind I cannot fight...eventually I'll go, but in order that I won't be pulled under I've got to prepare. Every time, I shout, 'I'm not ready, leave me be!' and if I think of something else I'm okay." Other entries during this period include the comments, "I know certain things must be done, like a robot I obey," and "I feel like a messenger. I have always felt my purpose, but I never knew it."

Much of what she received came not in words but in images and concepts. There was one statement, however, in which the words were clear: *I am I. I am many. We are many. I am not.* Amy said this statement was a sort of "riddle" about the Council. "It referred to my existence as an individual (I am I), my union with all minds (I am many), my absorption into the Oneness (We are many), and my identity as One (I am not). It is repeated often in my diaries. It's sort of like an 'oath,' 'pledge,' or understanding."

It is also quite reminiscent of messages given to Lisa and Anita, the *They are you–you are them* told to Lisa and the *IRU–URI* communication Anita received during a "question and answer" meditation.

Amy continued to have the training-session dreams, recorded in volumes of journals, in which she was shown how to perform levitation, affect electrical systems, and move through solid objects.

Looking back through the journals, she turned up a wealth of evidence showing the long-term involvement of unknown forces in Amy's life. Some of these details, in spite of her insistence that she had no recollection of being abducted, did indicate probable alien activity in the midst of it all.

Indicators of alien involvement such as time gaps and UFO sightings were in her journal and in her memory, although she had downplayed most of these events. Besides the missing-time episode and the small crouching figure she'd seen at age seven–which was accompanied by her eye being matted shut the next morning–there was also an incident at age fifteen of an unexplained physical presence intruding upon her.

Staying with her niece one night, Amy felt there was "something" in the bedroom before she went to sleep. She turned the light back on to look, but no one was visible. After going to sleep, she had a strange, frightening dream about a family trying to reach the spirit of a dead relative, and when the people in the dream started screaming at one point, Amy started screaming, too, and woke up.

"I felt someone kicking or jabbing me in the back, the whole bed was shaking, the canopy was flapping, and I felt someone/something in my room again. I ran...to my mother's room and told her, and she kissed me and said it was just a bad dream." It was so upsetting, in fact, that she refused to sleep in that room for two weeks.

Other suspicious dreams were recorded through the years, including two in 1977 that hinted strongly of an alien encounter beneath a screen memory. Amy said she dreamed "of being called out of my house by a small boy standing in the wooded park" nearby. "He took my hand," she said, "and we walked into the park at night."

The description of the second dream was more detailed. "I just dreamt a 'lady-doctor' gave me a shot, a tranquilizer," she noted in an April 1977 entry. "Then she disappeared and in the next dream I was being hypnotized. A man whom I seemed to trust and several other people I could barely see were standing around me. The man was so gentle; he told me to relax and somehow telepathically he explained [that] the dream I had earlier of receiving a tranquilizer was sort of a pre-hypnotic suggestion to relax me for the next dream. He then hypnotized me. I don't remember the rest, but my feelings in the dream were that of reaching out to those energy forces I call the Council."

This one was the most intriguing dream to date. In some ways it seemed to fit the screening phenomenon behind which abductions are often hidden, but it also seemed to have a very actual and "human" element to it.

That was not the case, however, with a dream Amy recorded on May 27, 1981, and it was here that the indication of alien activity became palpable. "I had the most unusual dream the other night," she noted. "I don't ever remember dreaming such a dream before. My body was floating horizontally through the house. I've dreamt of flying before and such, but always vertical and always mixed with unreal elements. But in this dream I knew I was asleep and I floated through my bedroom door, through the kitchen, turned the corner and floated into the back porch. I saw the walls go by, and each detail was as it really is. I began to note the lack of unconscious symbols as in a dream and felt alarm. I became frightened at the moment I felt it was not a dream. I felt suddenly sucked back into my bed – through the wall?!"

Amy drew a picture of the scenario as she'd remembered it in 1981. "Of all the dreams I've ever had," she wrote, "I'd say that was not a dream! It seemed real, it looked real, and it felt real. I don't know how, but I know I woke up exactly at the point I drew in the picture. I remember going through the window in the back door... I remember going up through the tree limbs. That's all I remember until I felt 'sucked' back into my bed."

The details of her "dream" were exactly like those reported in many abduction onsets, and this, coupled with the earlier possible missing-time episode and other indicators, pointed to alien involvement with Amy.

She had a conscious UFO sighting the following year, in July 1982, when she was living in the north Texas city where my family and I had also lived–at the same time, in fact, though unacquainted with one another. When she first mentioned this sighting to me in an early letter, she skimmed over the incident, saying merely, "I think I've only seen a UFO (actually five UFOs) once when they flew over my apartment years ago." I asked her for more details when we met, but her account was not much more specific. She said she was outside in the daytime when she saw the five craft approaching, and that she had called out to a neighbor to look at them, too, and then had walked around her apartment still watching them.

But later, Amy told me that "something weird" occurred during that discussion. "I didn't tell you, but it has bothered me since," she said. "I remember seeing the UFOs coming toward me as I sat in front of the apartments. Then they flew, slowly and without any sound, directly overhead. That part is still vividly clear. I realized what they were, and I got excited. I yelled at the guy in the apartment nearest to come see them. Then I walked along under them, directly under them...and I never took my eyes off them.

"But when I reached the back of the apartments, my memory is all messed up. Up to that point, everything is crystal clear...but after I went to the back of the apartments, I have two sets of memories. I remember watching them fly off slowly, but I also remember getting binoculars or my small telescope and looking at them. I didn't have binoculars at all. My telescope was still packed away."

Unfamiliar with the screening practices employed during abductions, Amy couldn't understand how there could be differing memories of the same time span. One 'memory track' contains the conscious parameters of the event: initial sighting of the UFOs, calling to her neighbor, walking toward the back of the apartments, and seeing the craft fly away. What is missing from this track is the continuity from the point where she sees the UFOs directly over her, to the point where she is watching them depart–a missing-time episode.

The second 'memory track' apparently provided a filler for that time gap. This memory tells her that she watched the UFOs through either a telescope or binoculars in that interim, which would have necessitated her going into the apartment at some point and unpacking a box to get the telescope, or getting binoculars, and going back outside, where her conscious memory picked up again. But this clearly didn't happen in reality, no matter what the second memory track told her, for the box was still packed and she did not even own binoculars. Something else happened in the time gap which she was not allowed to recall correctly, which is standard operating procedure in an abduction.

The event was confusing to Amy, as were the dreams she occasionally had of waving farewell to a UFO. In one such dream from the winter of 1988, she was with her daughters in a field behind their apartment, waving goodbye to the UFO. "When I woke up in bed," she said, "I was still cold from being outside. I got up and went to make sure the kids were back in bed, that's how real it seemed to me."

In all of these previous events and dreams and memories, Amy had recalled nothing about actual

192

aliens or being inside a UFO. The dream of November 1992, however, where she clearly saw the gray, masked female "non-Earth representative," took her, reluctantly, to a much more intense level of recognition that the alien phenomenon was a part of her life.

And when Amy realized how numerous and complex the unusual events had been since her childhood, she decided to explore some of those memories through regressive hypnosis. As a counselor, she was familiar with the theory of regression work, but she had never experienced it.

Amy arranged to meet with Barbara Bartholic in the summer of 1992 and went through two regression sessions, hoping to learn more about the part of her life that had been kept from her. In the first regression, they explored some early childhood and adolescent memories, but it was extremely difficult for Amy verbally to relate much of what she recalled in the trance state. It became apparent that Amy's response was inhibited by a severe block against talking about her experiences, especially when she was able to remember a threat made to her by a Gray when she was very young. In that fragmented memory, the Gray told her that if she told anyone about the visit, her cat would be killed. Amy did try to tell her mother, however, and the kitten subsequently died, although today Amy is reluctant to believe the death was a deliberate act by the aliens.

She also briefly remembered an experience a few years later, of a huge craft of some sort hovering just above her father's garden. She told Barbara that she was looking at it very closely, wanting to push it away, but somehow she received a clear impression that said, "Don't touch." Amy said she did not want to go into the craft, but she was taken inside, where she saw the same Gray who had threatened to kill the cat.

"I saw myself talking to someone inside it," she said. "I wasn't supposed to tell. This 'guy' telling me they would kill my cat was inside it. We were near the doorway, and he was taller than I and his face was right up in my face."

Next, she and Barbara explored the memory she had at age fifteen of something jabbing or kicking her and the bed shaking. "During the session," she said later, "I saw myself going to the back door. I couldn't understand because I looked sort of ghost-like and I was floating, not walking." As she tried to look at this event, however, that same scene kept repeating, of her going to the door and reaching for the knob, and she could not get past that point. "I guess it was too hard to look at," she said. "I remember the actual feelings of something in my room and being kicked or jabbed in my back–it felt so real. It was terrifying!"

The third episode they explored involved a childhood "lesson" about religion. "'Churches are not God'," she reported being told, "'statues and pictures are not God. Priests and nuns are not God. Nobody sins.' That doesn't make sense."

"What else did they tell you?" Barbara asked.

"To look beyond the pictures," Amy replied. "It's all lies. That made me mad, that all nuns and the priest were lying. Why did they tell me that when it's not true? They said Jesus was something like a soldier or something, supposed to lead people in some kind of direction."

"What did they want you to know?" Barbara

persisted.

"That I'm not supposed to [believe]," she said. "I can pretend to be confirmed. I have to pretend that I believe it, say the prayers."

In the second session, Amy retrieved a brief recollection of another "dream" encounter with a Gray she had in April 1993. "I had dreamt that some UFOs were picking people up here and there," she told me later. "Certain people, not at random. I stood and waited for them to come, I was supposed to wait. They shined a bright light on me, and then I was in the ship. First, I was facing a very shiny surface, like mirrors, then I turned around. I saw a lot of Grays at some instruments or controls, very busy.

"One Gray turned to face me, and I knew him. In fact, he was the same Gray I saw [in November 1992] in front of the moon or light. We talked with our eyes. I felt that he and I were very close once, we had been together once somewhere, and we had been the 'same.' It was like we were twins. I actually missed him! I wanted to go back to 'before' because I was remembering something. He told me I was to 'stay here.' I guess he meant in the present."

She also described the identity she felt with the "twin" alien. "I felt that I was one of them," she said, "and I was thinking of Barbara as 'a human with a mouth.' It was like looking through the eyes of a Gray! If I think of it as I am–human–they seem cold and uncaring. If I remember the way it felt to be one of them, in the dream, it is not cold, not uncaring, just the way it is."

In the hypnosis session, Amy could see the two of them in the bedroom, engaged in telepathic conversation, and feeling an old kinship with the entity. When Barbara asked why the Gray was there, Amy said, "I'm not supposed to know."

"Ask what you are supposed to know," Barbara suggested.

"He said in the next decade people will be expected to think the same," she reported, "being taught to think the same, like them. Make them easier."

Expanding later on what she was told, Amy said that in the coming decade the aliens doing the abductions would also promote a program in which people will be "taught to think the same. The sad part was that everyone will think it's normal and it is their idea. Even being an 'individual' will seem real but not in actuality. He and other aliens are trying to stop the process. It's been going on for a long time already."

Under hypnosis, as Amy tried to explain this information, she suddenly said, "He tells me to remember the rules. I'm trying. He was trying to help me remember. *Departure from the program will result in synapse damage*. It's so hard, without words, with words."

"What was that about?" Barbara asked.

"Do what you know to do," Amy parroted the statement of rules from the Gray, *"be human, be what you are.* Rule number two: *No memories*, rule number two."

These "rules" were given to Amy very early in her experiences with unidentified entities, and they always included a program to inhibit her talking about these events. An entry in her journal at age seventeen records one of the "rules": "I must not repeat previous mistakes." Amy said the mistake she was not supposed to repeat was the "mistake" of

196

telling her mother about the things she had experienced.

The first time as an adult when she tried to tell someone else, external interference stopped her, as the journal entry for December 16, 1979 shows. "I was writing a letter to my boyfriend tonight," she recorded. "I was listening to the radio. When I began writing of the difference between what the heart feels and what the brain knows [a lesson imparted to her by the Council], the radio began emitting every tone tolerable and intolerable to the ear. I was about to say something in a letter. I cannot remember what I wanted to say." The interrupting noise contained "voices, in unison, in some (foreign?) language."

Under hypnosis, Amy constantly had difficulty talking about the events, and she often repeated the rule against "telling." When Barbara tried to discuss the implanted blocks later, Amy was doubtful and couldn't accept the idea of the Council programming such an inhibition. It wasn't until she searched back through the old journals and saw entry after entry about not "talking" that she finally acknowledged the evidence of possible programmed control.

Her memories of the November 1992 dream-event were much more detailed, and easily discussed, as if the programming were ineffective, at least to a point. She penetrated several screens, recognizing that the large spider was actually a floating probe device in the room with her and the human figures she'd recalled. She also realized that she was with them and the spidery probe, for part of the encounter, in her own apartment.

But the most important information to emerge concerned the implants. When she described the flesh-colored object removed from her ear, she told Barbara that it was used as a transmitter and monitor. Amy said that the masked alien also explained the purpose of the implant she removed from the spine.

"She said that it short-circuits and it can kill!" Amy said. "They can kill as many as they want. It's in the neck. It's old, but some people have them. When they want to kill them, they...I don't like that thing. It does many things."

"What other things?" Barbara inquired.

"They make people like puppets!" Amy exclaimed. "She says they can control anyone that way. Bunch of damn robots walking around. But they're taking them out. They're old. Sometimes in the base of the spine, real low, but that's only half of the control. The other half controls up and down. Up to the brain or down the body. Old. They use something else now."

"Where does the new one go?" Barbara asked.

"Cerebellum," Amy answered.

"How do they put it in?"

"Not in the back like the old ones," Amy replied, pointing instead to a spot behind her ear. "You couldn't take it out, only they can. They can make...the people with the new ones and old ones in them...do what they tell them to do. If they don't, they do other things, switch them like puppets, switch them off. They can kill them, or turn it, many different degrees....they can use it as punishment, take away control but leave consciousness, or control the consciousness. Or they can kill. I'm mad!

"On one end it can kill, the other end, control, and in-between levels. Punishment is in the middle where there's consciousness but no control. Repetition, over and over, the fear takes over, and they don't have to punish any more. Fear is paired with punishment, so they don't have to move the switch so far. Fear and control. And if that doesn't work, they switch it to kill. When the body stops, it disintegrates all implants. Electrical activity ceases. Huh! That's gross but funny. They use our own brains as the batteries...feedback loop like a generator, through the implant and circuits back. When the circuit is broken, the implant dissolves. Little, like a Tic-Tac."

"How many people do you think have implants?" Barbara asked. "Is there a selection?"

"Whoever responds to fear, in any degree," Amy replied. "They test you. She says they tested me for the fear, nuclear holocaust fear [referring to numerous nightmares]. I did good, became afraid. I was wondering how they found me. Oh, follow the signal. The old ones they can follow easily. They changed to new ones, changed the signals, those buggers. They [the abducting and implanting aliens] know they're [the 'apologetic' alien-human group] out there taking them out, and they don't like it. That's why they change them sometimes, put in a different signal."

"Who does this changing?" Barbara asked.

"The others...other tribes?" Amy tried to explain.

Barbara asked her to describe these others, but Amy was focused on something else. "She says it's here in a year," she said, pointing to her forehead.

"What is there in a year?" Barbara asked.

"What I'll need, tools," Amy answered. "Focus, very important. She say's I'm not ready yet, to know. In a year. She said I'll remember the three guys standing over there. They're watching. They're not regular. They can talk with their eyes. Don't know if they learned it or what. The silver-haired one, [and] one with glasses."

"Are they alien?"

"Some. Their eyes, they wear contact covers. Without them," Amy explained, "they're slit, but they look like people. Not cat's eyes, too big. A line. He says he's a lot like me anyway. Gray-silver hair, he's the main one. He's telling me to forget them. Six feet tall, average build, regular shirt."

"How about his face?"

"Kind of not thin, not fat, right size for the body," she said. "The eyes don't fit." She indicated that the man had a widow's peak hairline. "Coarse hair," she said, "average length, like an average businessman. He could be one, with those contact lenses. He's nice."

"What about the other two men?" Barbara asked.

"He said, *Don't look.* He let me look at him but not at them. One has on contacts, though, I saw that. Brown, dark eyes but no pupil or iris or center spot, if people look closely. That's why they sometimes wear tinted glasses."

"How do you feel about these guys?" Barbara wanted to know.

"Sad," Amy told her. "They used to be where I was, manipulated by them. They don't want to tell me too much because it was more than I can take. That's why he says to look away."

"Are all humans manipulated?"

"Not all."

As difficult as it was for Amy to speak freely in a trance state, out of hypnosis later she described the things she'd been unable to articulate. She gave detailed descriptions of the scene in the dining room, where she saw the probe accompanying the three men. After being introduced to the masked alien, she was next aware of being taken into a large, underground room. She was led by two beings into the room, noticing the rough rock walls that proved she was below ground level. At that time she lived directly across the street from a FEMA underground facility, and that facility had undergone a massive expansion, both above ground with numerous antenna arrays and new buildings, and below the ground as well. But there was no way of knowing if she were in that facility or somewhere else.

Amy sketched the room in the facility where she and the men were with the masked aliens. She had smelled a certain odor during the hypnotic recollection, resembling "polish remover," which came from "a black ribbed tube on the side of the room." The masked alien told her it helped the aliens present to breathe better. And when questioned about evidence of a military atmosphere in the facility, Amy said she didn't observe any.

She had more to say about the humans, too, especially the silver-haired leader she nicknamed "Ol' Slit Eyes." "Ever since the hypnosis session," she remarked, "the image of Ol' Slit Eyes has stayed with me, vividly. Once you 'talk' that way, you always feel the link. I get the feeling Ol' Slit Eyes is either in our government or some high position in the military," she added. "People see him every day but don't know who he really is."

As for the other two men, she said, "The feelings I got from those three guys was deep sadness. They were designed like we are. They were watching me 'talk' with Ol' Gray and assessing how I handled the information and my 'loyalty.' It was just a feeling I caught from them."

Concerned about what she remembered being told of the implant's placement and functions, Amy went to medical texts for information about the cerebellum and medulla oblongata, the locations identified for the implants. She learned that the medulla is a switching center for nerve impulses of the higher brain centers controlling vital functions such as temperature, pulse, swallowing, and breathing.

The cerebellum was identified as the control source for muscle tone and equilibrium, as well as voluntary movements, coordination, and even the vocal cords–which, Amy noted, might explain the physical difficulty some abductees experience when trying to discuss their encounters. The information corresponded with the controls the masked alien said were functions of the implants.

After the November 1992 dream-event, Amy continued to recall several other dream-memories. She had sudden flashback memories and also witnessed more overt evidence of alien intrusions. She had more dreams of moving through solid objects, one involving her daughters, and Amy said she was not "happy" about seeing entities with them, although she felt the tall beings standing there with them were "quiet," "wise," and "rather nice." She dreamed of being aboard a craft, again with masked aliens, who said that humans were going to be told "who and what they really are" as well as "the truth about everyone." In another dream, she was made to feel that the "government" was "going to kill" her for talking about what the government was doing to people.

During one "teaching dream" Amy woke up and

could actually hear the voice of the "lady" talking in her head. "It is not a dream!" she noted in her journal. "Tried to write what the 'lady' was saying, heard her say, 'NO!' and suddenly began forgetting. Tried to write fast but hand went numb. Very tired all day, took a nap–more teaching dreams."

One of the most disturbing dreams occurred in June 1993, where Amy said she "had the vivid sensation of being held still by wires or tubes going into my head." Everything about the dream felt real. "I was pissed!" Amy said. "I could actually feel something going into my head. I wanted to pull them out, but I couldn't get my hands up to my head, my hands wouldn't move.

"Then I heard someone say, in my mind, *You don't want to pull them out. You will hurt yourself.* With that warning I saw a clear image of what would happen if I pulled the things out of my head. I saw the wires/tubes coming out and pieces of my brain were stuck to them and dropped off onto the floor. I just had to be still until it was finished. It didn't hurt," she added. "I was just so mad at not being able to move my head. I've never had a dream like that before. I'm still made as hell!"

On the night of September 20, 1993, Amy experienced a time gap, and her record of the event in her journal is very typical of such reports. After first noting that the phone made a strange "beep" at 11:17 p.m., she wrote, "I was sitting here at my desk in my study, and I noticed that I felt funny all of a sudden. I've felt that sudden, brief anxiety feeling before."

Her daughter walked in at that moment, and Amy reacted angrily because the child should have been in bed by that time, 12:07 a.m. "Then I went back to my work," she wrote, "and I felt bad that I had yelled at Grace. A few minutes later, I heard a noise that sounded like the door knob of the front door being turned. I thought Grace was opening the door to look for me (when I take the dog out). I jumped up and looked out the little window on the front door, but Grace was not outside.

"I turned on the light, but no one was on the porch. I opened the door and looked out, but no one was outside. I thought it was strange that I'd heard that sound. I went back to my work in my study. Then I looked at the time, and it was 1:27 a.m.!! I couldn't believe it! I'd lost an hour and twenty minutes."

Seamlessly, the time gap had occurred, and she had no memory of any disruption. But other times she had flashback memories pop up suddenly, including one scene in which she woke up one night hearing the words, *Did you think it was all by accident?* The statement's meaning was clear, she said, "that the Earth is a giant zoo or experiment."

Other such "downloadings" of ideas and scenes included one of a "future world" our children will "inherit," a world that is "dying." On one occasion, the thought, *We were without form* played through her head repeatedly. Two other such thoughts were more disturbing: *Survival of the fittest. That's why wars are promoted,* one said, and the other repeated, *Death is the journey Home.*

She also recalled a lesson which showed how the aliens use "frightening images" through 'mental projections" to control humans. "Fear is the real enemy," she said.

In April 1993, Amy had her first taste of a

phenomenon all too familiar to abductees: the black helicopters. After the first one flew over her home she noted, "They really do exist–now I know what one looks like." Other such flights have occurred since then, frequently late at night with repeated circular passes above her home.

And like so many other abductees, Amy has reason to believe her children have been touched by the phenomenon. One daughter recently said her leg was tingling "the way it feels when you put it through the wall," indicating to Amy that the child might well have been receiving the same sort of instruction she herself had. Her other daughter described two types of "balls of light" she has seen repeatedly in the house. On is larger than a basketball and multicolored, and the other type is smaller, displaying a trail or tail of some sort.

Amy was very concerned about further evidence of her children's involvement after what she thought was a dream turned out to be highly questionable. In the first part, she was aboard a ship with several smaller Grays and two or three six-foot-tall entities. The Grays told her that human concepts of "Armageddon" were not correct. "I remember thinking that what they told me was nothing like anything I, or anyone, had ever imagined," she said. And while this occurred, Amy said she could feel the taller beings "directing" the lecture and that their mind was in her mind, an intensely felt presence that made her "want to cry."

It was similar to the intensity of the "lady" who taught her things, she said. "No matter how tough I consider myself to be, I wouldn't stand a chance against the Tall Ones," she emphasized. "I think they reminded me that they have me, body and soul, and always have had me."

In the next part of the dream, she and her daughter Grace were involved in a series of scenes and events culminating with a police car approaching them. Amy said it had very bright lights that were "not right for a police car." The policeman inside, whom she didn't like, spoke to her, but then she awoke from the dream when her other daughter began coughing. She later went back to bed, hearing a "loud static-buzz sound" before falling asleep.

The next morning while cooking, Amy said her ear began to itch. "I rubbed my finger in my ear and felt something inside and outside of my ear. I looked at my finger, and there was some dried blood on it. I went to the bathroom and looked in the mirror. I could see dried blood in my ear and down my cheek."

Frightened that this had something to do with the strange dream, she carefully questioned her daughters to see if their night had been disturbed. Grace said she'd had a weird dream, and Amy began to tell her about the dream she had. When she reached the part about the colored lights on the police car, Grace finished the sentence for her, describing them as "like a rainbow." Amy asked her how she remembered seeing them, but Grace couldn't explain.

Amy's memories and the children's various remarks indicate alien contact with the entire family, although Amy is more convinced by the "hard evidence" and conscious experiences she has witnessed. Grace's recent spate of nosebleeds, for example, are a worrisome indication of possible implant activity, and Amy has further been mystified by certain unexplained scars on her body, including the circular scar on her shoulder and a one-inch linear scar down the middle of her nose that appeared in late 1993. This sort of evidence–as well as her conscious daytime UFO sighting in January 1994, of four objects merging into one–are all unwelcome because they make it difficult for Amy to reject the phenomenon's reality.

She knows that it is more than a question of random abductions, from the information she has been shown, and she is concerned about the direction and nature of events indicated by the information.

In November 1993 she recorded a vivid dream in which she was with other people in a large room. "We were told that we were selected to experience the end of the world," she wrote. "God was this ball of light that looked like a little sun. God was telling us that what we experienced was for all...that we should feel honored and lucky to experience the end of the world."

It was explained that Amy and the other humans were really "spirit beings" seeking challenging experiences. "Our true nature is to seek every opportunity to grow and to learn. Even sadness, sorrow, pain, and misery represent opportunities to experience and learn. I understood that the meaning of life was just to experience, that's all–experience."

This message resonates with another communication Amy has had from her unseen guides, telling her that humans are "a species within a species" and that our bodies are mere "containers" for the spiritual entities we truly are.

Another piece of information came in a conscious flash or vision, in which it was explained that a particular person would be coming to public notice claiming to be Christ. Amy said she was shown how all the religious people around the world would perceive this person as the incarnation of whatever deity they worshiped, and that he would be accepted as god on earth. This would cause many people to turn against those who didn't accept the new figure, leading to the persecution and suppression of what is actually true. In effect, she explained, the false leader and his false religious teaching would win out over spiritual truth.

A startling encounter in January 1994 had caused Amy to wonder even more about her lifelong involvement with the "Council." She heard about a very strange group of people, who called themselves the "Total Overcomers" or the "Omega" group, holding meetings in the Dallas area. Two of her acquaintances attended the meetings, and from the details they reported, Amy decided to invite the "Overcomers" to hold a meeting in her city, which they did. At that meeting, they told Amy and others attending that they had just emerged from their "classroom" after eighteen years of preparation under the total guidance of their twenty-four elders. Now they were traveling through the country to "harvest" the people who had been "implanted" with the proper knowledge and who were ready to make the transition to the next stage of "more than human."

This required breaking all human ties of love, family and friendship–bonds that keep us tied to the material world–as well as living in celibacy and surrendering all decisions to the "elders." They also said that everyone but their group had been warped and programmed negatively, either by society's false values or, in cases of alien contact, by "Luciferian" aliens–which included all groups except the one that had originally instructed the "elders."

Amy described the four "Overcomers" whom she met as tall, thin, pale, asexual in dress (black clothing) and hair style, "clone-like" in appearance, and rigidly controlled emotionally. In fact, she said that she could not feel any "souls" in these four people. Their message was equally rigid: followers must go with the "Overcomers" immediately, without a word to their families, with no belongings, and without any clue as to where they will go next.

These cultish demands were weird enough to Amy, but the truly disturbing aspect of the "Overcomers," she said, was the details and phrasing of their tenets given by the "elders," for they echoed exactly the things that Amy has been taught by her "Council." And the products of those teachings–in this cult, at least–felt extremely wrong.

"After all I've been learning about implants and mind-control," she told me, "I must ask who the Council really is. I am so afraid of them now. What if they have been programming me all this time to do things someday that may not be good for my planet? They have never told me to do anything contrary to my beliefs before, but what if they are just gaining my trust? What if they really are good and teaching me to help my planet and I stop listening to them? What if they are just some defense mechanism and all just my imagination? Somehow I'd rather be crazy than for it all to be real. So, since I don't know who or what the Council really is, I am listening to them more cautiously. I just keep asking God to help me find the Truth. God I am sure of."

X

KΔRLΔ ΔNĐ CΔSEY

After asking these eight courageous women to share their experiences with the public, it is only proper that I also give an account of the things my husband, Casey, and I have witnessed since the first year of activity recounted in INTO THE FRINGE. We have repeatedly been asked about further experiences, and the following summary will serve to fulfill that request, in addition to increasing the body of knowledge upon which research depends.

The first intense period of dealing with alien activity lasted from late 1987 through most of 1990, but after that the encounters dramatically waned in our daily life. We breathed a figurative sigh of relief, hoping that the aliens had moved on to another task. Besides, having become active in abduction research, this relatively peaceful period allowed us to focus on learning from other people's experiences, expanding our base of knowledge from the personal level to that of general society.

I still kept a calendar notation of any questionable or unusual events, but the frequency was so low that a journal wasn't needed any longer. In all of 1990, for instance, I recorded signs of only eight possible events, only three of which were evinced in a conscious or objective manner. In addition to some unexplained body marks, I witnessed another UFO sighting on February.

Leaving a friend's at 8:15 p.m. I saw a huge, white object flying rapidly at a very low altitude above three tall towers in the city. Driving on, however, I lost track of it, but when I reached my own neighborhood I saw it again.

I decided to go to the hill near our house and have one more look. When I parked and walked to a prominence to get a wide view, I immediately saw the same light coming from the west toward the south. It was moving much more slowly now, and bobbing along rhythmically instead of in a smooth, straight path. It passed between the downtown skyline and me, so I knew it couldn't be more than a mile away.

It began to grow larger, as if moving closer, and I felt ready to confront it, at last, in full consciousness. But after a bit, the light receded, still bobbing, and continued on into the south. I ran down the hill to the car, thinking I'd drive home for Casey and bring him back to see the object. Then I thought I should have one last look to determine where I would likely find it visible when we returned. So I raced back up the hill and looked around. The light was not where I had previously seen it.

I turned back in disappointment, and then caught sight of it again, in the very position it had started from the first time. The bobbing light silently repeated its path, once again coming close for a time and then backing away. I returned quickly to the car then and drove the half-block distance to my home. The streets were deserted as I pulled into the garage.

When I ran inside and yelled for Casey to come with me, he looked up puzzled from the couch and

211

asked if I had pulled into the garage twice.

"No, of course not," I replied. "Why'd you ask that?"

"Then I guess it must have been a truck out on the street," he said. "But it sure was loud, for just a truck."

"What are you talking about?" I asked.

"This huge noise," he said, "about thirty seconds before you came in the garage. It was so loud that the whole front of the house shook, like some huge tanks or trucks were barreling down the street."

"I was just on the street," I objected, "and there was nothing out there. But I did see a UFO, up on the hill." We drove together back to the prominence and were disappointed to see nothing but the usual air traffic in the sky.

At no time during 1990 did either of us have a conscious encounter, just signs that something might have been going on. Emotionally and intellectually, we had nothing concrete with which to deal.

In 1991, however, at least in the beginning, that was not the case. Both Casey and I felt a great, undirected stress, as we'd done back in 1988, and that experience told us that activity might be recurring which was kept repressed from our consciousness.

In January, our son's friend James reported encounters with unusual entities, one of which once masked itself with the illusion of a beautiful blonde woman before revealing a very different physiology. Casey also recalled a possible encounter with the blond group that month, which had seemed like a VRS dream event (as recounted in INTO THE FRINGE). For Casey, the event was disturbing and puzzling, and we both wondered if anything further

212

would occur. But nothing similar happened, nothing but a few unexplained marks, until April.

Shortly before leaving for the Ozark UFO Conference early that month, we had a "phantom sedan" incident, reminiscent of "Men in Black" reports. In this event, a very real-looking black car rolled down the street, came to a near stop as it reached our yard boundary, and a human-looking man in a white shirt and dark suit, wearing sunglasses, peered through the car's deeply tinted windows into the front of our house–where I was standing staring back out. I turned around to shout for Casey to come see it, and when I looked back the car had vanished.

In June, the mysterious helicopters returned, appearing on three different days. By the end of the month we made a permanent move to Arkansas, and thereafter, in an area with heavy, normal helicopter traffic, it was impossible to tell if any of it was unusual. We found a few questionable marks on our bodies in August, but it wasn't until October that a memory of anything specific turned up.

During the night of the fourteenth, I physically got out of bed at some point, and I also had a dream that aliens were about to come into a long, narrow room where I was waiting. My only thought was, *Don't scare me!* But nothing more remained in my consciousness, in spite of the bruise on my arm and scratch on my abdomen in the morning.

One other incident, in January 1992, involved another almost-conscious realization that an intrusion was occurring. I woke at 1:34 a.m., opened my eyes, and wondered why the room was so foggy. My immediate rationalization was that my eyes just hadn't yet focused, and I got out of bed to go to the bathroom. When I started walking, a sudden rush of thick, clear liquid with tiny black specks suspended in it flooded from me, much more than can be produced naturally by the body, but I had no idea where it had come from. Neither could I account for the new scratch and bruise I found the next day.

These things were physically real, yet something within me didn't really "come to grips" with what might be happening to us. I wouldn't let these events obsess me or throw me off track from researching other people's situations. If the aliens wanted to get my attention again, they were going to have to do a lot better than this, I decided. A strange snippet of a dream now and then, a few marks, even the liquid–the significance of which I certainly knew from other women's accounts–weren't enough to frighten me or move me in any serious way. I refused to feel under attack, even granting that some activity was occurring. But I was only able to keep this frame of mind because I wasn't perceiving them consciously.

For months thereafter, neither Casey nor I noticed anything inexplicable or suspicious. Throughout most of 1992 I was busy with radio and newspaper interviews, the result of INTO THE FRINGE being released, and I also worked on a research project involving Ted Rice, the well-known psychic in Shreveport, Louisiana, whose lifelong experiences with alien forces shed extraordinary light on some of the abduction activities which have been so hard to penetrate.

The period of no unusual activity, however, came to an end with a bang on the morning of October 13. I was sitting at the coffee table working on Ted's material, when a large ball of white light appeared and exploded right in front of me, less than four feet away. There was no noise, so I realized I hadn't merely seen a reflective flash from an explosion.

Five minutes later, a noise did occur, a very loud, pounding noise that slammed against the kitchen wall with a house-shaking thump. My dogs started up, barking, and we ran to the kitchen door to see what had happened. The garage doors were closed and locked, however, with nothing out of the ordinary in sight. My immediate response was a feeling that this was an announcement of some sort, a declaration of a renewed presence. And from past experience I could recognize the "feel" of this intrusion. There was no fear or anger in my mind, just a complete determination to face whatever would come next.

That proved to be a UFO sighting. On October 27, at 7 p.m., our neighbors phoned to say they'd been watching a UFO for the past ten minutes and wanted us to come out for a look. I had dinner cooking just then, but Casey and a visiting friend raced up the road, in time to watch an odd orange-red orb of light disappearing behind the tree line. The neighbors said they saw the orb change colors from white to orange, and that at one point a solid-looking beam of light emerged and moved around before retracting back into the UFO as it moved away.

Since this event was multiply witnessed, we didn't feel it was "aimed" at us. UFO sightings are surprisingly frequent in central Arkansas, and they are often seen by multiple witnesses. This sighting, although momentarily exciting, was oddly unaffecting. If this sighting report had come from someone else, I would have recognized the pacified response, but it's much harder to analyze oneself than someone else.

The next month, as I started a dusk stroll up the drive, I had my most bizarre UFO sighting to date. And again I experienced a sedated reaction. In absolute silence, a large, rectangular craft soared over my mother-in-law's cottage, which is thirty feet from our house, just above treetop level. My first response was exhilaration, and I started to run up the drive to follow it. But its speed, while not startling, was fast enough that the craft was soon out of sight, blocked by the tall, thick trees on our property.

I observed it long enough to get a clear picture, though. It reminded me of a train boxcar in length and width, although not quite as tall, and it looked metallic-brown. The bottom of the craft had an indentation or bar across the middle, with a large amber light at each end. Four more amber lights marked each corner of the rectangular object, for a total of six lights.

Within a matter of seconds, my exhilaration disappeared along with the craft, and instead of racing inside to get Casey, I just began to stroll again. When I did go back in, I told him of the sighting and that I hadn't had time to notify him before the craft flew off. My natural excitement and curiosity felt artificially suppressed, so much so that I didn't even make a notation of the sighting on my calendar. In fact, it simply faded from my memory for almost two weeks before I suddenly remembered it again. After experiencing this response several times, I am now convinced that it is externally imposed and thus denotes outside contact of a very real nature.

At the time, however, I was unconcerned. My

friend Brenda was in the midst of much more overt alien intrusions in her home, and they seemed more important than the few things we'd experienced ourselves. Besides, as I'd decided earlier, it would take something highly significant to pique my interest and get me to interact on a personal level with the aliens again.

On January 8, 1993, it got rather personal when I woke up to find my clothing had been removed, and I hadn't been the one who removed them. This was always upsetting to me when it occurred in the past, for it made me feel intimately and helplessly violated. I had the same response this time, and when I phoned Brenda to discuss it the next morning, she told me of the dream she'd had the same night. I was in it. She dreamed she was aboard a craft, immobile on a table, and she could see me on a table beside her, also unable to move. She said she tried desperately to reach out to me, but couldn't, and that's all she recalled. I had no memory to match the event, but the missing clothing was indicative of some nocturnal activity I hadn't generated.

It was Casey's turn next, in February. On the morning of the seventeenth he told me that in the middle of the night, at 12:38 a.m., a loud "bang" noise awakened him from a dream. (Normally I am the one who awakens at any sound, while he sleeps through everything.) In the dream, he had been standing in the living room looking out the picture window at the ridge behind our property. A large, white orb appeared in the sky and then descended to the ridge. He told me that he instantly remembered the dream when he was awakened by the bang and that he then got out of bed and walked into the living room. Just as in the dream, he stood peering out the window, watching in full consciousness as a large, white orb appeared and descended to the ridge.

"What happened then?" I asked, and he shrugged.

"I guess I went back to bed," he said, "but I honestly don't remember doing it." And his response was curiously passive, as mine had been. This time I noticed and determined to be more alert if anything else were to occur, to fight the passive effect in order to react the way I thought best, rather than the way some outside force directed me.

In April I also had a nighttime event, much less dramatic than Casey's sighting of the orb, but nonetheless inexplicable. At 1:14 a.m. I awoke hearing the sound of a C-130 airplane, with which I'm very familiar as training flights from the nearby military base have regular paths over this area. The plane sounded as if it was just coming directly overhead, at an extremely low altitude. My first reaction was irritation at the thoughtlessness of training flights at such an intrusive hour. *I'll phone the base in the morning and complain,* I thought as I lay there with Casey soundly asleep beside me. But seconds, and then minutes, elapsed, and the noise of the C-130 didn't waver, increase, or diminish.

It can't be hovering! I thought, but that's exactly how it sounded—as if a C-130 was motionless low over the house. In a normal state of consciousness—which I really thought I had—I would have awakened Casey to hear it, too, but I didn't. Instead, six or seven minutes after first hearing it, I just fell asleep. It didn't occur to me to resist.

For over a year I had kept the attitude that I wouldn't acknowledge alien contact back in my life, in our lives, without strong, overt experiences. I had also been praying, in my fashion, to whatever good and loving and true higher forces may be out there, asking for two things: that they guide me to know and follow the power of goodness; and that they communicate with me in an overt manner, without any subtlety or ambiguity. I prayed for help, for information that would be clear enough for a child to understand, as I realized my level of understanding and perception were about that rudimentary in dealing with the aliens. I wanted a communication that couldn't be dismissed, variously interpreted, or ambiguous as to its nature.

On May 10, 1993, I may have gotten a partial answer to that prayer, although great caution is called for in assessing any contacts before accepting them at face value. This particular contact conformed exactly to other abductees' descriptions of the VRS dream and was the first of its kind I had experienced to such a degree.

I was in the middle of a normal dream when suddenly I was somehow removed from that dream and found myself sitting in a chair, in a darkened area, accompanied by entities I wasn't allowed to see. They spoke to me, clearly and frequently, throughout the event. I was facing a small stage area, which I now feel was more holographic than solidly three-dimensional even though at the time it looked quite realistic. My "hosts" told me I was to watch a scenario played out on the stage.

It began with a scene from Genesis, in which Esau returned home feeling so hungry he feared he would die. His younger brother Jacob was sitting there eating a bowl of pottage, and Esau begged him to share it. Jacob said he would give Esau the food, but only in exchange for Esau's birthright as the oldest son of Isaac. I heard Esau say, *It won't do me any good to have the birthright if I die of starvation, so I'll agree to trade it for the food.*

Then the scenario on stage changed to another part of the brothers' story. In this second scene, Isaac was very old and blind and knew that he was close to death. He called for Esau to be brought to him to receive the laying-on of hands that would confer the inheritance. Jacob wrapped an animal skin around his arm and presented it for his father's touch. Isaac felt the fur and believed it was the arm of his very hairy eldest son. So in his ignorance of this deception he conferred the blessing and gave Jacob that which rightfully belonged to Esau.

The play ended, and then it started right up again, playing out several more times as my hosts discussed its meaning with me. At various points they would stop the action, much as we pause a video tape, and would point out some specific detail and tell me what it meant, what it symbolized, and what the message was trying to convey.

They told me not to focus on the biblical aspect of the play, that their message had nothing to do with any actual Jacob and Esau, but that the story was designed to illustrate important information about what the aliens are doing to humans, both in the past and in the present. The hosts went through the play with me several times, pointing out details and saying things like, *Okay? Let's try it again. Now watch closely.* And the play would proceed.

After several repetitions, I suddenly "woke up" in my bed, amazed by what I'd just seen. I got out of bed for a while, trying to discern the nature of the event, whether dream-like or externally generated, and I also pondered on the meaning of the scenario. When I lay back down, as soon as I touched the pillow I was suddenly back in the chair, facing the stage, and my hosts said we would now resume. Once again the play began running, as did the explication offered by my abductors. And when they apparently were satisfied, the action ceased and the abductors gave me a clearly delineated summary of the things I was meant to perceive.

Esau, the older and hairier brother, they explained, represents the original human species on this planet. Jacob represents the altered product of alien genetic manipulations of that older species. The aliens produced this new variant and then used it to replace the original form.

In our current situation, the aliens are once again doing genetic alterations of our species and are once again trying to produce a variant which will be more useful for their purposes and which will supplant us. And again it will be attempted through deception, as Jacob deceived Isaac. This deception, I was told, is being carried out by the aliens through exploitation and manipulation of global events, including weather phenomenon, to make us believe that the planet is in imminent danger of cataclysm and destruction.

This is why they impress the idea of coming destruction upon so many abductees, telling then they will have tasks to perform at that time. They want us, as a race, to be so afraid of this upcoming destruction that when they show themselves openly and offer to save us in some way, we will be willing to take their help, even if it means giving up our birthright, so to speak, which is preeminence on this planet. Like Esau in his hunger, we will say, "What good does it do us to keep our birthright if we're all going to be destroyed along with the planet? What have we got to lose if we accept alien help, even though that means accepting alien control? Better to survive under subjugation than not at all."

But my hosts stressed that this is all a deception, that our planet, without their intervention, is not in imminent danger. These terrible disasters we see–the flooding, hurricanes, and earthquakes–are sometimes being intensified by the very aliens who will then come in and offer to save us from "inevitable" destruction. We should not believe them, I was told emphatically. And we must not surrender our sovereignty to them, as that would mean we were truly lost forever.

After this, I knew nothing more until waking in the morning, very disturbed by what I'd been shown. I had no way of identifying the source of this event and never caught even a glimpse of my abductors, who stayed behind me in the dark. I couldn't deduce anything about the event from my past encounters, because this one was completely different. I knew I hadn't been taken anywhere, because I woke up consciously in the midst of the experience and was able to check my physical surroundings. And there was no doubt in my mind that during the encounter I was not asleep; in fact, I remember being so awake when I was removed to the chair that I thought, *How can they snatch me right out of a dream like that?*

The experience seemed designed in some ways to fulfill the request I'd made for a straightforward, clearly comprehensible communication that would be helpful. They must have taken me at my literal word, for the message was reinforced in every conceivable way: visually, repetitiously, and verbally. So did that mean I could accept it as coming from a benevolent source? Could I test or trust its accuracy?

All I could do, finally, was hold the message in reserve and compare it to the events that occur as time passes. At least parts of what they told me I already knew to be true. The aliens do make a practice of giving abductees information about a coming time of destruction or change. With the many natural disasters of recent time, it is an easy message to believe. And they have engaged in what appears to be genetic processes for years, according to abduction accounts, as well as taking credit time and time again for the creation of the human species. But even these two "facts" I still had to question, because in neither case could we objectively verify the activities.

Things around our home went back to normal after that, until the middle of July, when a series of odd noises started to plague us. We heard everything from large plastic ware (nonexistent, of course) shattering on our wood floors, to gigantic invisible woodpeckers hammering away in the living room. Things got even stranger one evening in August, when Casey and I had a parallel and infuriating experience. I heard him ask me a question, and when I turned around to answer him, instead he answered it himself. Both of us heard the other one ask the question, it turned out, although neither of us had even been thinking about the subject.

Throughout August and September, there was an undercurrent of tension in our lives that felt just as it had back in 1988, after alien contact had renewed with Casey but before he was consciously aware of it. His usual coping mechanism for work and personal concerns seemed impaired, so that almost every interaction was stressful.

The stress was affecting me, too, leading to recurrent insomnia and sleep disruptions. I started doing something I've never done in the past–leaving my bed, and Casey, to try to rest elsewhere. Sometimes I'd lie on the couch, with the dogs nearby on another couch, and sometimes I wrapped up in a blanket and slept fitfully on the guest bed. There were no conscious events to show that anything suspicious was occurring, but the insomnia was not normal, and neither was my willingness to be separated from Casey.

We weren't in step with each other or comfortable with ourselves in those weeks. I became worried as the situation seemed to go on and on, but I couldn't pick up any clue from Casey about his thoughts. Given all that had happened in the past months, I should have asked him if he thought the stress indicated suppressed memories of new contacts. But I was honestly afraid to ask and risk a confrontation with something that felt so heavy or ominous.

It was Casey who broke the silence, one night as we drove home from visiting friends. In the quiet of the evening drive, he began to talk after a long period of silence, seriously and very tentatively. I could feel he was searching for a way to be both confiding with me and reassuring of my feelings at the same time.

What he told me were the details of two dreams. The first one had occurred in early September, but he hadn't told me at the time. When the second one occurred later in the month, however, he had described it to me the next morning. I recalled he said we were a team of detectives in the dream, and then he sketched out the details of our pursuit of two suspects. We had chosen to follow one of them, a woman, but when we caught up with her we realized she was innocent, that the other suspect was the guilty party.

"I think it was a symbolic message," he told me that morning. "I think it was telling me that you and I are on the right path in this work with the abduction situation. We're following the truth, that's what the beautiful woman we caught represented."

In our talk in the car, Casey began by telling me about the first dream, from early September, and I could see why he'd been reluctant to discuss it.

"Something's been going on," he said, "and I want to tell you about it. I had a dream earlier this month. It woke me up, and I looked at the clock. It was around 4 a.m. I thought there would be plenty of sleep time left so I wouldn't be tired when I got up for work. Satisfied, I rolled over and started to drift off, when I remembered what the dream was about. And I noticed then, and only then, that my heart was still pounding faster than usual.

"I thought there must have been something to that dream, so I tried to remember more. There was a strong odor of spicy sweat and a stronger scent of fear in the dream. I think I was nude, and so was this woman who was sending out fear and pain signals. She seemed to be very confused and upset by the situation. I felt dazed and angry, dazed by whatever control was being exerted on my mind to get me into this situation, and angry at being in the situation in the first place.

225

"I felt pity and sorrow for her, so I held her gently and tried to calm her down. I tried to talk normally, and that seemed to reassure her and give her back some sense of control. When she calmed down, I awoke. And immediately, I remember now, I smelled the air to see if there was any scent from the dream left on me. But there wasn't."

"Did you recognize the woman?" I asked. "Do you know her?"

"Yeah," Casey said, naming a casual acquaintance with whom we've never had any social involvement. "I really tried to think it was just a dream," he said, "and that maybe I was going through some sort of mid-life mental quake, but I don't think that's it. Anyway, I didn't tell you about it because I didn't want to worry you. But after the second dream, I can't keep this quiet any more."

"Why?" I asked. "Was it something awful?"

"No," he said, "it wasn't a bad dream. Do you remember me telling you the dream where we were detectives?"

"Yes," I replied, recalling the conversation quite clearly.

"Well, that was the dream," Casey continued. "I told you about it at breakfast, and we talked about whether it was symbolic. And I really thought it was. Until two days ago."

"What happened?" I asked.

"I was at the mall with a friend for lunch," he said. "We had eaten and were heading around to the escalator, and then this woman came around the corner, dressed all in black. She was blonde, genuine blonde, and her skin matched the color, eyes, too. She looked at me, started to lift up her arms, and said, 'H-

226

h-hello!' And then she seemed to get real confused and walked on past me."

"What did you do then?" I asked. "Did you go after her or talk to her?"

"No," he said, "we went up the escalator , and when I got to the top I turned and looked back down there. She was still there, looking very disoriented, and then she walked off slowly."

"So what did that have to do with the dreams?" I wondered.

"That woman in the mall," Casey said, "was the same woman I saw in the detective dream. That was her! In the flesh! I recognized her immediately, and I swear she acted like she recognized me, too. You know how you'll reach out to hug a friend you haven't seen in a long time? That's how it was, and when she reached for me I was starting to reach for her, too."

"What do you think is going on?" I asked. "What does this mean?"

"I don't know," he replied. "I thought that was just a dream, but there was the real woman. So now I don't know if the first one was a dream, either. And that was a bad situation."

"Do you remember anything specifically sexual happening in the first one?" I asked, thinking of the encounters in other abductee reports.

"I didn't see anything like that happen," Casey told me. "I only saw us kneeling in front of each other, nude and scared and angry. We were in a circle of bright light that came from somewhere above us, and everything outside of that was too dark to see. But I sensed it was a very large room. Something could have gone on, either before that or after, and I just don't remember."

"How did you feel, while it was happening?"

"I didn't feel sexual. It was more a very deep sorrow because that woman was in such terrible panic and fear and pain. It was so thick I could almost grab it in the air, all that emotion. All I wanted to do was make her feel better, give her some comfort, and that's what I remember doing. Just holding her and talking."

"Have you seen her, I mean in person, since the dream?" I asked.

"Yeah," he said.

"So how did she seem? Did she say anything?"

"No, she didn't say a word. I passed her on a stairway, and she looked at me very intently. I think her face even turned red, and then she looked down at the stairs and went on by."

"Does she usually say hello when you see each other?"

"Yes, she's always been friendly in the past," Casey said. "I don't know why she acted like that, unless that whole thing wasn't really a dream. But there's no way I can ask her about it, we don't know each other that well at all."

"And we don't have a clue as to finding the woman in the mall," I remarked, wishing we could ask her if she really remembered the incident in Casey's dream.

"No, I never saw her before," he said. "But we had a connection, when we were looking at each other, a very strong connection. I looked at her, and then it was like I was inside her head, her eyes, looking back out at myself. And I could feel her, in a way, that she really is good, a good person. She's not responsible for whatever might have happened. If anything really did."

That was the question we were always left to face, the nature of an event's reality. In some reports, two people have separately recalled being in an identical dream or situation, and in those cases the people involved can feel more certain of the dream or event's objective reality. But it doesn't always happen that way. Sometimes one person will have a traumatic experience involving another person, and the reality of the event is so convincing that the experiencer believes the other person was truly involved, no matter how impossible time and location considerations may seem.

Granted, there is plenty of evidence for the aliens' ability to manipulate time and space, so the objective reality of such events cannot automatically be dismissed. But there is also hard evidence that the aliens are masters of illusion, total-sensory, gut-and-heart-wrenching illusion, generated by an external mechanism. And when an abductee is in an altered state, the illusion is very convincing to his controlled perceptions.

This lesson had been brought home by the extraordinary VRS involving Amelia that Ted and Marie witnessed in 1991, and now I was seeing, possibly, with my husband's bewildered emotions, just how masterful the aliens' deceptive mechanisms can be. For Amelia, the event had been a virtual-reality solo flight, the external product or result of the blue sphere technology and its creators. Knowing this, I wondered if Casey's dreams were objective or virtual experiences, the product of some similar technology, and so did he. The only thing he knew to

229

be "real" was the nameless woman he came face to face with in the mall.

This experience, all of our experiences and those of the eight women recounted here, define the abduction phenomenon. It is complex, ambiguous, deceptive, inconsistent, traumatic, physical, and metaphysical, with no single or clear purpose. There are patterns and possibilities, but none so plainly verifiable that everyone can agree on the facts, much less the larger truth, of the agenda.

If all that Casey and I knew about alien abductions was limited to our own experiences, we would have a very different picture of the situation. And we would be much more vulnerable to alien manipulations or programming in our ignorance. It is only when we consider our experiences within the larger context of Amy's experiences, and Beth's and Lisa's and the experiences of the thousands of other abductees, that we gain enough knowledge to get past the personal illusions. And it is only by giving up our wishful ideas and facing the data squarely that any of us can hope to penetrate to the actuality of these events, to come to terms with "what is" rather than what we wish it to be.

COMPARATIVE
CHART
OF
EXPERIENCES

CONTACTS:	Polly	Pat	Lisa	Anita
UFO Sighting	•	•	•	•
Childhood Missing Time	?	•	•	•
Adult Missing Time	?	•	•	•
Conscious of Encounter	•	•	•	•
Virtual-Reality Scenario	•	•	•	•
Remote Telepathic Communication	•	•	•	•
Other Family Experiences	•	•	•	•
Group Missing Time		•		
ENTITIES:	Polly	Pat	Lisa	Anita
Gray	•	•	•	•
White	•	•	•	•
Robed/Hooded	•	•	•	
Blond Hair	•	•	•	
Reptoid/Brown	?	•	•	•
Cat-Eyed	•	•	•	
Wrinkled Face	•	•	•	
Dwarf/Elf	•		•	
Miscellaneous			•	
Blue			•	•
"Jesus" Figure		•	•	
"Hybrid" Adult	?		•	?
Black	•		•	
Red Uniform				•
EXAMS:	Polly	Pat	Lisa	Anita
Miscellaneous Instrument	•	•	•	
Close-Up Face	•		•	•
Physical Inspection	•	•	•	
Ear Implant	•		•	
Gynecological	•	•	•	
Nose Implant		•	?	
Head Surgery	•	•	•	

232

CONTACTS:	Beth	Jane	Angie	Amy
UFO Sighting	●	●	●	●
Childhood Missing Time	●	?	●	●
Adult Missing Time	●	●	●	●
Conscious of Encounter	●	●	●	●
Virtual-Reality Scenario	●	●	●	●
Remote Telepathic Communication	●	●	●	●
Other Family Experiences	●	●	●	●
Group Missing Time	●		●	
ENTITIES:	**Beth**	**Jane**	**Angie**	**Amy**
Gray	●	●	●	●
White	●	?	●	
Robed/Hooded	●	●	●	●
Blond Hair	●	●	●	
Reptoid/Brown			?	
Cat-Eyed		●	●	●
Wrinkled Face		●	●	
Dwarf/Elf		●	●	
Miscellaneous	●		●	●
Blue			●	
"Jesus" Figure	●			
"Hybrid" Adult			●	●
Black				
Red Uniform			●	
EXAMS:	**Beth**	**Jane**	**Angie**	**Amy**
Miscellaneous Instrument	●	●	●	●
Close-Up Face	●	●	●	●
Physical Inspection	●	●	●	
Ear Implant	?	●	●	●
Gynecological	●		●	
Nose Implant	●	●		
Head Surgery	●			●

233

EXAMS, continued	Polly	Pat	Lisa	Anita
Wand Instrument			•	
"Lady" Doctor		•		
Missing/Taken Fetus				•
Black Box				
Saw Surgery on Human			•	
Made to Eat or Drink			•	
Miscellaneous Implant	?			
ACTIVITIES:	Polly	Pat	Lisa	Anita
Information Communicated	•	•	•	•
Teaching Abductee	•	•	•	
Levitation		•	•	
Baby Presentation	•	•	•	
Pass Through Solid	•		•	
Sexual Activity	•		•	•
Alien and Human "Merge"	?			?
Testing Abductee	?	•		
Telekinesis		•		
Abductee Work UFO Equipment	?	•	•	
See Clone		•	•	
"Celebrity" Present			•	
View of a Past Time		•	•	
Immersed in Liquid			•	
COMMUNICATION:	Polly	Pat	Lisa	Anita
Chosen/Special Abductee		•	•	
Discuss Human Origins		•	•	
Spirit-Body Separation	•	•	•	
Warning of Disaster		•	•	?
Strange Word		•		•
Specific Name Given		•	•	
Singing/Music	•	•		
"Don't Touch UFO" Warning			•	

EXAMS, continued	Beth	Jane	Angie	Amy
Wand Instrument	•		•	•
"Lady" Doctor	•		•	•
Missing/Taken Fetus	?		•	
Black Box	•	•	•	
Saw Surgery on Human			•	•
Made to Eat or Drink	•		•	
Miscellaneous Implant	•			•
ACTIVITIES:	Beth	Jane	Angie	Amy
Information Communicated	•	•	•	•
Teaching Abductee		•	•	•
Levitation	•	?	•	•
Baby Presentation	?	•	•	
Pass Through Solid	•		•	•
Sexual Activity			•	
Alien and Human "Merge"			•	•
Testing Abductee	•		•	
Telekinesis		•	•	•
Abductee Work UFO Equipment			•	
See Clone			•	
"Celebrity" Present		?	•	
View of a Past Time				•
Immersed in Liquid	•	•		
COMMUNICATION:	Beth	Jane	Angie	Amy
Chosen/Special Abductee	•	•	•	•
Discuss Human Origins			•	•
Spirit-Body Separation		•	•	•
Warning of Disaster	•			•
Strange Word	•	•	•	
Specific Name Given		•	•	
Singing/Music	•			•
"Don't Touch UFO" Warning			•	•

SETTING:	Polly	Pat	Lisa	Anita
Humans Present	●	●	●	●
View of Desert World	●	●	●	
Military Personnel Present	●	●	●	?
Instrument Panel		●		
Computer/TV Screen			●	
Underground Facility		●		
Graph or Chart	●	●	●	
Animals Present		●	●	
Body of Liquid			●	
BODILY EFFECTS:	Polly	Pat	Lisa	Anita
Bruises	●	●	●	●
Triangle Mark	●	●	●	
Noise in Ear	●	●	●	●
Nauseous	●		●	●
"Light" Explosion in Head	?		●	
Scoop Mark			●	●
Clothes Mix-Up	●		●	●
Scratch Mark	●		●	●
Puncture Mark	●	●	●	
Rash				●
Miscellaneous Mark			●	
Feel "Beaten Up"			●	●
Sudden Total Fatigue		●	●	●
Blood on Body	●		●	
Blood on Bed	●		●	
Eye Irritation	●		●	
Body Vibrates			●	
Miscarriage				?
Hair Loss				
EXTERNAL EFFECTS:	Polly	Pat	Lisa	Anita
Electronic Disturbances	●	●	●	●
Telephone Disruption	●	●	●	●
Unknown Outside Light	●	●	●	●

236

SETTING:	Beth	Jane	Angie	Amy
Humans Present	●		●	●
View of Desert World	●	●	●	●
Military Personnel Present	●		●	●
Instrument Panel	●	●	●	●
Computer/TV Screen	●	●	●	●
Underground Facility	●		●	●
Graph or Chart			●	●
Animals Present	●	●		
Body of Liquid	●	●	●	
BODILY EFFECTS:	**Beth**	**Jane**	**Angie**	**Amy**
Bruises	●	●	●	●
Triangle Mark	●	●	●	●
Noise in Ear	●	●	●	●
Nauseous	●	●	●	●
"Light" Explosion in Head	●	●	●	●
Scoop Mark	●	●	●	●
Clothes Mix-Up	●	●	●	
Scratch Mark		●	●	
Puncture Mark	●	●	●	●
Rash	●	●	●	●
Miscellaneous Mark	●	●		●
Feel "Beaten Up"	●	●	●	
Sudden Total Fatigue	●	●		
Blood on Body	●	●	●	●
Blood on Bed	●	●	●	
Eye Irritation	●		●	
Body Vibrates	●	●		
Miscarriage	?		●	
Hair Loss	●		●	
EXTERNAL EFFECTS:	**Beth**	**Jane**	**Angie**	**Amy**
Electronic Disturbances	●	●	●	●
Telephone Disruption	●	●	●	●
Unknown Outside Light	●	●	●	●

237

EXTERNAL EFFECTS, cont.	Polly	Pat	Lisa	Anita
Unknown Inside Light		•	•	•
Unidentified Voices	•	•	•	•
Miscellaneous Sounds	•	•	•	•
Indoor Multicolored Light		•	•	•
Interior Hum or Buzz		•	•	•
Helicopter Activity			•	
Ball of Light			•	
Miscellaneous Artifact	•	•		
Clicking Sound	•	•	•	•
AFTEREFFECTS:	Polly	Pat	Lisa	Anita
Sleep Disruption	•	•	•	•
Desire to Live Rurally	•	•	•	•
Shift in Attitudes	•	•	•	•
Compulsion	•	•	•	
Dream of Many UFOs Arriving	•	•	•	•
Dream of Great Disaster		•	•	•
Sense of Task to Perform	•	•	•	
Prophetic Dream or Vision	•	•	•	
Fear Reaction		•	•	•
Block Against "Talking"	•		•	
PERSONAL:	Polly	Pat	Lisa	Anita
Psychic Experiences	•	•	•	•
Celtic Ancestry	•		•	•
Native American Ancestry	•	•		•
Gynecological Problems			•	•
Childhood Abuse				•
Family Member in Intelligence				•

EXTERNAL EFFECTS, cont.	Beth	Jane	Angie	Amy
Unknown Inside Light	•	•	•	•
Unidentified Voices	•		•	•
Miscellaneous Sounds	•	•	•	•
Indoor Multicolored Light	•	•		•
Interior Hum or Buzz	•	•		•
Helicopter Activity	•	•	•	•
Ball of Light	•		•	•
Miscellaneous Artifact	•		•	
Clicking Sound	•	•	•	
AFTEREFFECTS:	**Beth**	**Jane**	**Angie**	**Amy**
Sleep Disruption	•	•	•	•
Desire to Live Rurally	•	•	•	•
Shift in Attitudes	•	•	•	•
Compulsion	•	•	•	•
Dream of Many UFOs Arriving		•	•	•
Dream of Great Disaster	•	•	•	•
Sense of Task to Perform	•	•	•	•
Prophetic Dream or Vision	•	?	•	•
Fear Reaction	•	•		•
Block Against "Talking"		•		•
PERSONAL:	**Beth**	**Jane**	**Angie**	**Amy**
Psychic Experiences	•	•	•	•
Celtic Ancestry	•	•	•	•
Native American Ancestry	?	•		
Gynecological Problems	•	•	•	•
Childhood Abuse		•	•	
Family Member in Intelligence		•	•	

XI

EXPANDING THE VIEW

A comparison of the data from these separate reports emphatically proves one point. Our current concept of the abduction experience is too small, too limited, and far too simplified. The Comparative Chart lists 114 elements from the reports, including details which were omitted in previous chapters because of space considerations. When the data is categorized and correlated, some surprising consistencies emerge that force the current view to expand, in both quantity and quality.

Before beginning the comparison, however, it should be noted again that four of the women underwent some regressive hypnosis: Beth, Jane, Angie, and Amy, with three different hypnotists. Out of the 114 listed details on the Chart, Beth reported 87, Jane reported 77, Amy 73, and Angie had 96. The other four women showed consistently fewer reported details, although not significantly so. Polly had 67 of the 114 details in her account, Pat had 71, Lisa had 94, and Anita reported 53. Almost all of the details, from each of the eight women, came from pre-hypnotic recollections.

In the "Contacts" category there are eight different situations reported, and seven of these eight have been reported by all of the women. These include

UFO sightings; missing time as a child; missing time as an adult; consciousness of an encounter; virtual-reality events; telepathic communications; and the extension of alien involvement into lives of other family members. Three of them experienced missing time or abductions with other people.

The data indicates, then, that the phenomenon is not imaginary or self-generated, that it is linked to the UFO sightings, that it involves a generational interest on the part of the aliens, and that contact can be made by remote means.

The "Aliens" category contains a surprising variety of physical types reported, including some that are rarely mentioned elsewhere. While all eight women encountered the Gray aliens, the Whites (insectoid) and the hooded figures are almost as common, turning up in seven accounts. Blond humanoid figures have been seen by six of the women, as have the cat-eyed or reptoid type. Half of the women reported a wrinkle-faced entity similar to a tall Gray or White, as well as a shorter, often hairy creature variously referred to as a "troll" or "dwarf." And both a blue entity and a "Jesus" figure have been witnessed by three of the women.

In addition to noting the variety of physical types, it is important to realize that every combination of these different entities have been reported working together in abduction scenarios. It is hard to conclude, then, that the various types are really separate groups carrying out separate functions or missions.

Abductees typically report undergoing some sort of physical examination at one time or another, as researchers have long acknowledged. A comparison of the details reported in the "Exam" category show that two areas of the human body are most commonly involved: the reproductive system and the brain. Only five of the women remember gynecological procedures, however, and only three of them report possible implanted or missing fetuses, so the aliens' interest in reproduction or genetics may not be their sole purpose. While this group comprises all women, they are not the only sex reporting fetal implantations or extractions, as bizarre as this seems. In one man's account, he recalled an abdominal incision into which a malleable sac of tiny fetuses was placed and later surgically retrieved. Another man said that a similar fetal container was inserted rectally.

More of the women report implant procedures and "head operations" than gynecological activity. Anita is the only one who does not recall receiving an implant, and five women report some surgical activity on their skulls or brains. This activity has no apparent connection to a crossbreeding agenda and points to a program of greater complexity than the limited "genetics" theory.

A variety of alien instruments are reported in these procedures, but the most common here are the wand-type device, found in four accounts, and the small metal box, usually black, which is reported by three women.

There are four accounts of a "lady doctor" present during examinations, and three of the women saw operations performed on other abductees during their experiences. Three also were made to eat or drink something while in alien custody.

The most common detail of the examination scenario, however, is the report of an alien's face very close to the abductee's face, which has been experienced by all of the women but Pat. Whether this is a type of examination or an exertion of mental control over the abductee isn't clear, and of course it could be both. There is evidence that the large, black, glassy eyes so familiar from Gray reports may not be biological eyes but instead may be coverings that perform technologically, able to calm the abductee, do a scan of some sort, and even, as Pat felt, "film" or record data from our minds.

Other activities besides the exams occur in abduction encounters. All of the women report that the aliens communicated with them at some point, although not during every encounter. And seven of them recall teaching or testing sessions. During abductions, six report experiencing levitation, five recall passing through solid objects, and four witnessed or performed telekinesis. On the 'hardware' side of things, four women were shown how to operate some of the equipment aboard a craft, and on the 'software' side three of them were induced to relive or envision a past time or event in their lives. Again, these activities point to an agenda more complex than crossbreeding.

Six of the women do, however, report scenes generally known as "baby presentations" in which apparently hybrid infants are shown to abductees and are said to be created from some human-alien crossbreeding process. But half of the women also report being forced or induced to engage in (mostly traumatic) sexual activities with aliens, humanoids, or other abductees. And all these activities have little to do with crossbreeding or gathering of reproductive material.

Some researchers have theorized that all such

sexual scenarios are the product of mind control–erotic images without substance–used merely to facilitate an actual event which involves nothing more than the taking of sperm or ova. But there are problems with this theory. For one thing, although sperm-gathering can be accomplished via erotically induced orgasm on the part of a male, it certainly isn't necessary for ova-gathering. In fact, it is totally unnecessary. Nor does it serve a reproductive purpose for her to be compelled to masturbate, as in some abductions, as well as in cases where the person feels "switched on" for this purpose when no abduction is underway. Another problem is that sexual intrusions involving reproductively immature children are reported. And finally, there is clearly no sperm/ova gathering going on in those situations where abductees are forced into sexual situations together.

Abductees report a wide yet consistent pattern of communications from the aliens, both in their presence and through remote contact. The most common communications focus on the origin of the human species, the "special" nature of the alien-abductee relationship and of the abductee personally who has an important function to perform, the distinction of body and spirit, and warnings of future global destruction, which were all reported by a majority of the women. These are not trivial subjects. It would be as dangerous to ignore this information as it would be to believe everything the aliens say.

In the "Settings" category there is a similar consistency of reports, including the highly controversial scenario of the underground base, present in half of the cases. Even more surprising, perhaps, is that seven of the women saw other apparently human people in their encounters, working with the aliens aboard craft as well as in the terrestrial facilities. And in six cases, the humans were perceived as military personnel.

Many researchers have, unfortunately, been unwilling to take reports of human-alien collusion seriously. One researcher told me that he believed every case of human collusion could be explained as illusions perpetrated by an exclusively alien group. But all it takes to dispel this view is one confirmed case of military or human involvement, and from information that has been shared with me in confidence, I am satisfied that at least one such case exists, that of Leah Haley, whose ordeal of military intrusions and threats is told in LOST WAS THE KEY.

Another researcher has claimed repeatedly that none of his many investigations has produced reports or evidence of human military involvement. His claim, however, has been disputed by some of the abductees with whom he has worked, who say they have indeed reported these events only to have them discounted by the investigator.

Yet the reports overwhelmingly point to actual human involvement with alien abductions. Details of reports are consistent throughout the country, and the only thing that differs, finally, is the interpretation of those details by the researchers. Reports of human military involvement must be addressed with more than an unexamined dismissal, for they are as common as the baby presentation scenarios that are accepted at face value by the traditional view. Whether "real" or contrived, these events serve a purpose that the researchers need to discover.

Six other accounts described the abductees either viewing or being in a desert setting or on a desert-type planet, although the explanation of this scene varies from one report to another. Within the alien facilities, five women saw television-type screens, four saw instrument panels, and four were shown graphs or charts. And although it isn't noted on the Chart, three women described unusual black, flexible tubing in the facilities, both aboard the craft and in underground locations.

Other reported details in alien settings included bodies of water or liquid, in three cases, as well as three reports of animals present. Of more concern are the three accounts of abductees seeing, or being told of, cloned human bodies. Both Lisa and Pat were shown clones of their bodies, although they were given different explanations. Similar reports come from other abductees, and in one case a man said he saw a room full of inert male and female human bodies, who were beautiful and identical. The implications of such reports are enormous, considering the possible uses the aliens could make of these carbon-copy human bodies.

The eight women reported a number of physical effects, consistent with general abduction data, but the only two effects which were universal were patterns of unexplained bruises and particular noises in the ear or head. While the noises could be rationalized, perhaps, the bruises clearly indicate some physical interaction. The repetition of triangular marks in abductee reports may well indicate a single source for all of the marks.

Other signs of physical, rather than psychic or spiritual, contact include six reports of unexplained blood on the women's bodies or bedclothes, six reports of scoop marks, five women with scratches, and seven with puncture wounds. The case for actual physical contact is also bolstered by the six women who reported waking up with their clothing on backward, inside out, or completely missing.

The women experienced a variety of other physical reactions in addition to the internally heard beeps and electronic-type tones. All but Pat, for instance, experienced nausea during or after an encounter, and five reported sudden, total exhaustion in which all their energy drained away in an instant. Five women described awaking at times and feeling as if they'd been "beaten," to use Anita's term. And five said they had episodes in which a blinding light seemed to explode in their minds.

Unexplained rashes turned up in five of the cases, and instances of badly irritated eyes and waking with an unidentified bitter taste were both reported four times. Additionally, two of the women suffered unusual hair loss and unaccountable "sunburns."

The physical nature of the abduction scenario extends to other things in the abductee's environment. The external effects related to the phenomenon are very consistent, as the Chart demonstrates. Every one of the women have experienced bizarre electronic disturbances, for instance, and phone disturbances, both with the equipment and the callers. And seven out of eight reported lights in the yard, lights in the house, voices, clicking sounds, as well as miscellaneous thumps, pops, whistles, bangs, and hums in the environment, all without explanation. Outside the house, five of the women have witnessed the overflight of unaccountable, unmarked, or unidentifiable helicopters, all appearing after the abductees became aware of their situations.

The most consistent correlations between the women show up in the "Personal Response/Event" category. All of them suffer from chronic or frequent sleep disruption, all have undergone drastic attitude shifts, and they all feel a strong desire to live in rural locations, no matter what their previous backgrounds. Seven of the eight women report unexplained compulsions associated with their experiences, such as Polly's compulsion at times to take children, including other people's children, to a certain spot where UFOs are often sighted, something she would not do of her own choice. And Anita is the only one who has not reported feeling they are being prepared to carry out some unidentified task, job, or mission related to the alien agenda.

Three types of dreams show up in seven of the reports, as well. The first involves the arrival or landing or invasion of numerous UFOs on earth, a dream reported so frequently with the same details that I refer to it as "The Night of Lights," from the typical description. The second dream shows scenes of coming disaster and chaos on the planet, and in some cases the abductees are led to believe that their upcoming "jobs" will be carried out at the time of destruction. The third dream type is prophetic, showing events which come to pass after the dream.

The final category, "Personal Background," shows, in fact, that all of the women have demonstrated above-average psychic abilities. The data on ethnic background included here has only relative importance, focusing as it does on the Celtic and

Native American heritages which are more prevalent in American abduction reports than any other specific ethnic groups. The abduction phenomenon is global, and in any given region the ethnicity would surely be different. What is significant, however, is the high percentage of the women who have had unusual or serious gynecological problems, an indication that abduction experiences may be hazardous to their health.

The two remaining aspects of personal background, childhood abuse and a family member in the intelligence community, deserve special notice. Some researchers and mental health professionals, unable to accept the reality of this phenomenon, have offered screened memories of child abuse as an explanation for abduction memories. But as in the case of objections to military involvement, all it takes is one abductee who suffered no abuse to explode the theory. Among these eight women, only three reported childhood abuse of any kind, and their memories of these events were not repressed.

Other theorists believe that abduction activity is perpetrated by humans rather than aliens, carrying out massive mind-control experiments for some unknown purpose. They argue that the agents of this activity would have access to "subjects" through the families of those in the military and intelligence organizations. While it is true that most abductees have a family member in the military, that is also true of just about everyone in the country, so that cannot be a significant factor. More telling would be an inordinately high number of abductees with family connections to the intelligence community, and such cases are reported. Among the eight women, however, there are only two confirmed, and one possible, with connections to intelligence work.

These individual, very unique, abduction reports show such a commonality that they all could quite easily be from a single source, or alliance of sources, with a single, specific agenda. Some of the reported details, in fact, which appear so unique in a given single case, are too striking to dismiss. One good example not listed on the Chart involves Pat and Angie, whose conscious memories and responses are very different. During Pat's childhood abduction, she asked for and was given a "green healer rock" as a keepsake, but when the military interrogated the family, they persuaded Pat's sister to give them the rock.

In Angie's case, a green rock was also confiscated. She didn't consciously connect the beautiful green rock with alien experiences, nor could she remember precisely when and where she first got it. But Angie does remember, as a child, being approached on the playground one day by an unknown woman. The woman knew Angie's name and a few things about her, claiming to be a friend of the girl's teacher. After a brief initial chat, the woman told Angie that she knew about the green rock and asked if she could have it. Angie recalls giving her the rock during a second encounter, although the details are cloudy.

There are other such minute similarities in just these eight accounts, and the details on the Chart generally are true not only for the eight women but also for thousands of others.

There is one more set of parallels, however, which was not on the Chart because it pertained exclusively to the women in this project rather than to the typical abduction situation. I was in contact with all of them separately for months before deciding to compile a book-length report about the cases, and during that time, although strange things still occurred, they did not seem any different from past activities. Things changed, however, after Jane and Amy were given messages telling them to work with me specifically.

I began the book project, and in the course of taking care of necessary business through the mail, it soon became clear that many of my letters to the women were being diverted. It was an annoyance, but a minor one. But then the women began having serious problems, physical afflictions of a suspiciously similar nature.

Beth was first. On the night she decided to participate in the project, she phoned a friend to discuss the decision, but in the midst of the conversation the line went dead. That night, she had disturbing but cloudy dreams, and the next morning both her legs from knees to ankles were in excruciating pain for no apparent reason. And then she had a sudden, frightening flashback that linked the mysterious pain with military personnel warning her not to be a part of the book.

That was in early October 1993. Three weeks later, after discussing my determination to do the project with one of the women, I went to bed in fine shape and woke up at 6 a.m. with wracking, spasmodic pains in both legs, from my knees to my ankles. It was unbelievably bad, unlike any pain I've had before, and after swallowing ibuprofin I hobbled back to bed and tried to sleep. I must have, for I dreamed after that, seeing myself surrounded by military personnel who were injecting something into my knees. They taunted me, saying, "Don't think you can do anything you want. This is just a little demonstration that we can bring you, literally, to your knees any time we choose."

For Beth and me, these may have been mere dreams, reflecting our fears about the project. But Anita's report of experiencing this same pain after an abduction, years before, makes it harder to discount a connection. And on the same weekend I had the leg pains, both Anita and Jane suffered unexpected gall bladder attacks, so severe that they both underwent emergency surgery at almost the same hour.

Angie was the next to suffer. After an abduction in early November, she woke up with several physical symptoms, the worst of which was heavy congestion. It quickly grew worse, and in the space of less than two months she had to be hospitalized. Before that time, however, her health had been remarkably pristine. It was in November, too, that Angie recalls military personnel threatening punishment if she "talked to Karla Turner."

Was it a real event, a VRS, or just a dream? Anita had a similar dream shortly thereafter, in which I first discussed abandoning the project and then military personnel arrived and interrogated her about UFOs. Lisa, too, felt a very human threat against her involvement with the book and almost decided to remove herself from it. But in the end, all of the women felt that the information was too important to let intimidation, if that's what it really was, prevent its release.

To conclude, then, the Comparative Chart shows how consistently the same details turn up in unrelated abduction scenarios, and indeed how many consistent details actually comprise the phenomenon. Such reports demand that serious attention be given to uncovering the nature and extent of human activity within the abduction phenomenon.

The evidence further makes a strong case for a very physical, technological basis to alien-human interactions. Unless angels perform rectal probes, however, and make crank phone calls, and arrange sexual liaisons in addition to their other heavenly duties, the case is very weak for this being a primarily spiritual agenda.

XII

THE ROUND TABLE

When these personal accounts are brought together for an overview, the women have three major concerns, in common with many others who have had forced alien encounters. What are the aliens saying, and can we believe them? What are they doing with us, technologically and psychologically? And what is the real nature of human or military involvement in the abduction activities?

On this last issue, every one of the women have reported seeing other humans present in abduction situations. Amy, Angie, Lisa, Pat and Beth recall experiences that involved military personnel, and in most instances there were aliens working with the humans. Although some of these scenes may have been alien VRS productions, other peripheral activities do indicate actual human involvement. Angie, for instance, was confronted and intimidated by uniformed men in the pickups that pinned her between them on the highway, just hours before she had a military abduction and was threatened about "talking."

When Amy traveled out of state for regressive hypnosis, another suspicious event occurred. A high-ranking naval officer, a long-time acquaintance of the hypnotist's family, showed up at their home late on the night of Amy's arrival, in spite of being told that it would not be convenient to visit at that time. He proceeded to deliver the standard "line" that the military has no interest, much less involvement, with UFOs, aliens, or abductees. He said that in twenty-five years of service he had never even heard another military person mention UFOs, on or off the record. And he insisted that abductees had no business presenting their experiences to the public unless they could also offer "concrete, scientific evidence" that anything had happened.

I was present that night, and when I asked him if he actually could tell us of any military involvement with UFOs, assuming it did exist, he admitted that "national security" restrictions would force him to deny such involvement.

When Amy left to drive home, she was followed by a state patrol car who stayed inches from her bumper or right beside her car for many miles. The effect, of course, was extremely unnerving, and Amy felt it was meant to be an intimidation, as do those who have had military helicopter harassment, phone disturbances, and other events that seem much more human than alien in origin.

If, as was mentioned earlier, there is proof in even one case that military personnel have been involved in abductions, then the other reports should not be easily dismissed. Each person must decide what evidence is convincing on this issue, but I am satisfied that one case, Leah Haley's, is beyond question. If human agencies are indeed covertly active, their involvement demands more vigorous investigation than has been done up to now. Mainstream researchers, however, show no enthusiasm for confronting possible human-rights violations by human forces, perhaps because they fear personal reprisal–which, as many abductees can attest, does occur.

On the issue of alien communications, there is plenty of data from all of the women. Most of them have had personal messages in addition to hearing their names called. "The communication that has happened when I'm awake," Lisa reported, as an example, "is usually simple. They say in my head, 'Turn off the lights and don't come in here'." After Anita was sexually assaulted by the humanoid in the red suit, he told her, "I'll be there to help you," which was frightening rather than reassuring given the immediate situation. And Amy had a curious message in late 1993, saying, "All will know of UFOs on the day of the big game," although which big game was not identified.

Some of the personal messages, described previously, made direct references to me, once the women began working to investigate their experiences. Jane was told to give all her "information to Karla Turner" and to assist me in awakening others to the abduction phenomenon. Amy was compelled to contact me by her influencing forces, and then when she consciously asked them if they had any message for me, they told her to tell me, "Do take care. Lock your doors–it may help more than you know." The message was so absurd that Amy challenged it and was told, "She will know what it means." When Amy wrote me, she did not pass along that message, although she typed it and put it away.

Months later, when she was listening to a tape of a

public presentation I had made, however, she heard me say that at one point I was so disheartened by the alien activity that I didn't even bother to lock my doors. Shocked by the correlation, she finally told me about the message she'd gotten earlier. And when Polly asked her "spirits," as she called the unseen communicators, about this book project, she was given a lengthy reply. In part, they said that the book "is a journey into another level of mind" and that my books "are a part of a much larger work from which she cannot be separated...an expansive work of love, resting on a solid base."

It is impossible not to wonder what these specific personal references mean. They certainly show that some force or group is aware of the connections between the women and my research, which may account for the helicopter flights and telephone interference so many of us have had. During a phone conversation with Angie, in fact, as we discussed one alien group's claim to originate in Cassiopeia, a man's voice interrupted to say, "There's a lot of them out there, and we know where they come from"–and then the voice was gone.

These references also demonstrate foreknowledge of certain events or the ability to direct events, for whoever gave Amy the message about my locking the door seems to have known she would later, much later, hear a tape of my remarks. These specific references connect our separate experiences within a larger organized agenda, that much is clear, although the coordinators of this activity are not, and it seems to be quite a long-term project.

Many of the women had alien communications very early in their lives. Anita reported being told as a

257

child that "The children must be protected." Amy had messages and ideas impressed into her mind from as young as four, and like Polly she felt the impact of these influences in her early teen years. She also felt that the aliens implanted or stored information within the subconscious, in "packets" of knowledge, reminiscent of the "pockets" of knowledge the aliens told me I possessed in 1980.

Throughout their lives, several women recalled teaching or training communications. For Amy, these included information about various aspects of physics, as with Polly, as well as lessons in telekinesis and penetrating solid objects. Angie's training has focused on using her mental powers, and Anita's propelled her to study useful survival skills. This training or programming of abductees is meant to serve some purpose, but we have only the aliens' claims for what that purpose may be.

Much of what the aliens have communicated has affected the women's attitudes on a variety of subjects. In childhood, Amy witnessed an apparent VRS designed to destroy her faith in traditional religion, and Polly reported lessons on "changes in allegiance." Anita, Jane, and Amy also have come to feel suspicious of temporal governments, a suspicion that Jane says was "fostered" by the aliens. Such an attitude adjustment is clearly an intrinsic part of the abduction agenda, pointing to a much more involved and disturbing program than the mere taking of genetic material to revivify a degenerative alien race. Their actions concern changing our belief system as much as working, for whatever reason, with our bodies, and we do not know the motivation for this targeting of religion and government.

On the subject of human genesis, the aliens often say they are our creators, as in Angie's case, and statements about altering our species were also made to Lisa. The most provocative message, given to Amy, indicated a surprise on the part of the aliens that Amy hadn't clearly seen the situation already. "Did you think this was all by accident?" she was asked, as the aliens presented the concept of the earth as a cosmic zoo.

Such indoctrination serves to reduce our concepts of human sovereignty, as well as to bind us to them in a subservient position, as a possession. While some people accept this relationship as fact and thus allow that the aliens can legitimately do with us what they please, there are others of us who feel we possess an inherent sovereignty and right to exist without interference, no matter what our genesis. Their claims to be our creators have never been more than mere claims, anyway, unless there is proof somewhere, as a few researchers report from intelligence and military insiders.

As for information on the aliens themselves, they are less forthcoming. Lisa was told that there are "many divisions" of the beings, and Jane has observed that while some of them are interdimensional, as Polly also believes, others are actually "interplanetary travelers." An origin in Cassiopeia was stated to Angie, although the alien said their group had long ago made a "home" for themselves on our planet. Beth was told only that the aliens are here for study and to "avert a destructive process" that humanity is bringing upon the world. The most extreme communication of origin, however, was given to Pat. She was told that the aliens are angels, although not as we'd been taught to think of them, and that they will be responsible for the changing of human bodies at the time of resurrection. Jane, conversely, has been made to see, from her experiences, that the God of the Bible "is not the supreme being we have been taught to envision."

A common communication has been that the abductees are to come together or "find" others like themselves. In fact, Angie reported being brought to a group of "Chosen Ones" in an underground facility. "There were others trained like me," Amy said she was told in 1989, "and we would come together soon. Now it is time that we find each other." Beth was told that she and others must work as "spiritual" beings "for the good of humanity," and the aliens told Jane that "All good people of earth must come together to resist what is coming." It isn't certain, of course, that all the communications have come from a single source, and in fact there are frequently contradictions and inconsistencies from case to case.

The future planetary events are also a major topic for the aliens, and it is interesting to note the phrases and images they use here. For Jane, the aliens have used terms like "the awakening" to indicate coming changes in "world cultures and consciousness." This sounds positive and peaceful enough, but both Amy and Polly have been told of a coming "Armageddon," although Amy was told that Armageddon "will not be as people think it will be." Angie's abductors said that the "filth and evil" in this world will be cleansed as we are subtly changed. But for Anita and Lisa, the future changes are shown as disasters for which they must prepare to survive here on earth.

And Pat has been shown scenes of the return of

Jesus, accompanied by space ships and aliens, preceding the "bad time on earth" which will destroy many of those who are not rescued. Indeed, to Amy, Beth, Jane, and Polly, the communications have indicated a war of good and evil underway, in which we have a part to play. And as for the aliens' promised assistance, Lisa has said simply, "Why should we believe they can fix our problems when they can't even control the abusive aliens among them?"

How do the women feel about their alien communications? Jane is inspired by much of what she's told, but she has not been able to initiate the communications herself. In fact, she feels that the aliens have hidden, in a way, behind their contacts. "We're not seeing the true intelligence behind all these scenes," she once said. Polly says that when she considers all she has been told, she concludes that in reality, "They have told us nothing." And Amy has complained that in spite of all she's been told and taught, the aliens "don't give [practical] information."

Angie has come to be suspicious of much of what she has been told. "There's no reason I should trust those aliens," she wrote, "any more than I would trust my own kind." And Anita has echoed that feeling. "I'm always amazed when I get any information from them at all," she said. "I really don't know if someone who would abduct a person could be trusted to give a truthful answer to any question."

The second issue focuses on alien technology as observed by the abductees. Besides the various instruments used in examinations, most of which are completely foreign, it is curious to note how often the aliens employ quite familiar equipment, especially needles and injections. Indeed, some researchers have said that this use of mundane technology argues against an alien force and toward covert human activity. Angie, Beth, and Polly all report getting shots, and the other women have sometimes found injection punctures without remembering how they got them. But the most common technological devices are not at all human-like: the probes. Their descriptions are often very similar–small balls of light floating or bouncing through the house–but in Amy's case the probe was rather more "spidery" in appearance.

As mentioned earlier, there is a strong interest in human brains evinced by the aliens' activities. Amy, Angie, Beth, Lisa, Pat and Polly all reported having some operation performed on their brains, and they often used the exact same descriptions, of feeling as if their skulls were opened and their brains temporarily removed.

But by far the most alarming evidence of alien technology concerns the "new" bodies and "clones" they manufacture. Whether these are really bodies for a future human "resurrection," as Pat was told, remains to be seen, for other explanations have been given. In a case privately reported, for instance, a man was told that a duplicate of his body could be used to "replace" him if he didn't "cooperate" with the aliens. Lisa, too, was told that other people wouldn't be able to distinguish her cloned body from the original, if they chose to replace her. And Angie was shown the cloned infants as part of a "novel breed" the aliens are producing.

Polly has a different take on what may be going on with the baby presentations. "What's the point?" she asked. "Not to nurture this crossbred infant, not to teach the ETs about emotional love and physical bonding, but to blow our goddamn minds. They use our bodies to get to our minds and emotions." She doesn't believe they care anything about our bodies, "except that WE care very much, so that is why our bodies are important to them: to get at our caring."

This view is echoed by Angie. When she was shown one of her "hybrid" offspring, she felt that the presentation was a test of her rather than anything to do with the baby itself. "From that particular experience, I learned that the hybrid presentation liturgy is not a bonding exercise," she concluded. "In reality it is an act of scrutiny against the mother's measure of courage and understanding. It has a lot to do with mental pain and how the mother deals with it."

Concerning the clones or hybrids themselves, she was further told that their souls are "recycled" and that they are regenerated many times. This fits in with other reports in which abductees saw the aliens destroy fetuses and were told they are not "really alive" and that their physical material will be used, not wasted. In fact, these and other reports point to the use of human genetic material to produce the Gray workers, quite possibly biological "robots" rather than living, soul-inhabited, entities.

The other major technological question concerns the implants, for which the aliens have given various explanations. When Jane received an ear implant, she was told that it affects "brain chemicals and certain subtle functions." The aliens told Angie that the implants "act as a magnet and pull information from people's brains" as well as enhancing the use of "special senses" and sending "instructions."

But Amy was given very different information about the implants by the masked alien who removed hers. Besides being shown where the implants are placed and the fact that they operate on the abductee's own electrical brain activity, she was also told how the implants are used to control abductees, punish them, and even kill them.

And although no one was told that the implants are used to create the virtual-reality scenarios, that possibility must be considered. The technology behind the VRS is a subject upon which the aliens have been silent, but the effects of the VRS are apparent. Only Amy has been given any information about the images created by aliens, when she was told that they use frightening images for control. One of the aliens told Angie that the military also uses "illusions," but this was not explained.

Several of the women have their own ideas about what is behind the virtual-reality scenarios. Besides the control factor mentioned by Amy, Anita believes there may be a positive purpose for some of the VRS activity. "I suspect a lot of these encounters," she said, "are alien-induced dreams, for the purpose of making sure you feel comfortable with them." Lisa said, "I believe sometimes I'm made to dream odd things to see my reaction to them." And Jane, too, believes the aliens sometimes create frightening "set-up scenes, absurd stuff," which has made her uneasy. "I'm afraid," she confided, "we might find that intelligence [behind the illusions] so cold and impersonal that it would be unbearable."

Given all their experiences, what do the women themselves think about the aliens, their encounters, and the agenda to come? Pat is the only one who had unequivocally positive feelings and trust in the aliens–before her encounter with the "oriental girl" in the underground facility, that is–for her perception of them has been shaped since her childhood to see them as angelic beings. Jane, Angie, and Beth all recognize positive and negative forces among the aliens, and while Amy has been threatened and silenced through the years by the aliens, she still says, "I don't think all aliens are bad. I don't even consider the Grays that are abusing humans and other life forms as 'bad'–they have their reasons and think differently from us, so they probably do not understand our feelings."

Angie goes further, saying, "Perfectly real aliens exist out there, and it seems one kind wants to help us and another kind wants to deceive us." Anita has recognized differing agendas among the groups who have interacted with her. She thinks the Grays care very little about humans personally, the humanoids are involved with sexual aspects of the phenomenon (from her conscious recollections, at least), and the Tans are concerned to bind us to them through our emotions.

Polly has expressed many ideas about the alien agenda. "I know many feel they [aliens] need reproductive material from us," she wrote, "but the way it feels to me is, although there may be the aspect that we are a resource, it feels like a highly sophisticated mind game." And she recognizes, as has Anita, that the mind game can be very effective. "Intellectually I can say, 'They are out for control; don't trust them'," Polly has confided. "But, Karla, emotionally and deep in my mind I trust certain ones of them more than anything else in the universe. And I have been confronting bit by bit the evidence that they made me feel this way for their purposes, to fulfill their agenda, not for my good. The depth of my trust, I think, is more frightening than the depth of my fear." Like Anita, she recognizes the directed nature of her response.

"Their consistent theme is control," she continued. "It is maddening to realize that although we strive to empower ourselves and know that we can claim and enforce our own mental sovereignty, still so often they slip by our defenses...and own parts of us which by rights we should have in our conscious possession."

In spite of what some prominent abduction theorists tell us about avoiding thinking in terms of "good and evil" or "positive and negative" when it comes to the aliens, this simply cannot be done, nor should it be. For these women, for my husband and myself, for all abductees, knowing that we have been made a part of this agenda and that we have been implanted, trained, and programmed to participate in some future scenario, how can we not ask to what purpose our minds, bodies, and souls will be used? How can we put aside our rationality, our learned wisdom, and our ethics to trust the words and actions of beings whose nature is kept hidden from us and whose agenda involves the entire world?

More immediately, what can be done to alter the abduction situation? Is there any sign that things are changing? The answer is a cautious yes, there is evidence of a change in the 'standard operating procedure' of abduction events over the last forty or fifty years.

On the part of the aliens, there seems to have been a quantitative and qualitative increase in abduction activity since the mid-1980s in this country. Whereas most events in the past were deeply suppressed in the abductees' memories, by 1986 hundreds, if not thousands, of abductees began to remember past experiences and to be more currently aware of new ones. Either the aliens were not doing a good job of suppressing the memories, or something was triggering a wake-up call in the abductees. Further, more abductees were reporting a variety of alien physical types, not just the small Gray workers typically encountered in the past.

An argument can be made that this awareness was initiated deliberately by the aliens, as part of the preparation for the predicted coming global event in which abductees will be activated to perform their "tasks."

But a different argument can also be made, that abductees were waking up on their own, many times "seeing through" the illusions and virtual-reality scenarios as Anita did when she told the Tan entity who was projecting love toward her, "Too bad it isn't real." In several recent reports, in fact, abductees have penetrated the aliens' illusions and refused to cooperate as the aliens would have had them do. The growth and changes resulting from alien contact may yet prove to be a double-edged sword, giving abductees a heightened awareness and psychic perception that allows them to evaluate and react to their situations in ways they could not have done before.

It has been said that any species, in an environment of extreme stress and questionable survival, may develop new coping mechanisms to ensure that the species continue to exist. Could this be part of what is happening now? Certainly an intrusion of an advanced, controlling force on a widespread scale could generate enough "species stress" to trigger new response mechanisms.

Studies of human consciousness development theorize that the emergence of bicameralism–the division of the psyche into conscious and subconscious components–occurred relatively recently in human evolution, perhaps no more than five thousand years ago, in a fairly sudden way and with no known precipitating cause. Could it be that we are once again experiencing a psychic change, a movement toward "tricameralism" that will give us a new form of conscious perception? Are we developing new abilities to recognize energies and entities which have hitherto been beyond our ken, and thus new ways to respond?

Many people who see alien interaction as a positive event for humanity point to the growth and changes abductees often evince as proof that the aliens are working to elevate the psychic abilities of our race. Angie has said, echoing the reports of numerous other abductees, "I have grown in many ways. My IQ and receptiveness to learning has improved a lot, and I am more in tune to nature as well as myself and other human beings." Defenders of alien interaction claim that these sorts of changes are a deliberate product of the contact experience, evidence of the aliens' benevolent interest in humanity.

It is odd, however, that such growth seems to come to abductees only after they are aware of their experiences. If indeed this growth is produced by the aliens, then it should have been there long before the abductees were conscious of their encounters, since in almost every reported case there are signs of alien involvement since early childhood. The psychic increase and growth of perceptive abilities, however, occurring after the abductee is aware of the intrusions, may indicate a different genesis–an internal evolution of consciousness–stemming from our need to know what is and has been done to us and what we can do to meet the situation in a more empowered position.

Survivors of great catastrophes such as hurricanes, earthquakes, or war, may be crushed by the impact of these events, losing their usual ethical considerations and sense of self that is the basis of psychic stability. Or they may find a new resilience, rising to the occasion and reacting with abilities they didn't know they possessed.

Given the vast intrusive activities of the abduction phenomenon, we as a species may well feel such a threat or stress that a "mutational" or evolutionary leap is occurring today, developing a tricameralism of the mind, allowing us to confront the intruders and see them more clearly than they have allowed in the past. On the basis of many recent abduction reports, there is hope that our species is awakening.